D1462002

Dying
Well

WILLIAM D. BARNHART
1712 North Larrabee
Chicago, IL 60614

Dying
Well

Kenneth L. Vaux
and
Sara A. Vaux

Edited by Kenneth L. Vaux

Abingdon Press, Nashville

DYING WELL

This book is printed on recycled, acid-free paper.

Library of Congress Cataloging-in-Publication Data

Vaux, Kenneth L., 1939–
    Dying well / Kenneth L. Vaux and Sara Anson Vaux.
       p.   cm.—(Challenges in Ethics series)
    Includes bibliographical references.
    ISBN 0-687-10933-7 (pbk.:alk. paper)
      1. Death—Social aspects.   2. Death—Moral and ethical aspects.
    3. Death—Religious aspects.   4. Thanatology.   I. Vaux, Sara Anson.
    II. Title.   III. Series.
    HQ1073.V38   1996   96-26864
    306.88—dc20

Excerpts from *The Troubled Dream of Life* by Daniel Callahan are reprinted with the
permission of Simon & Schuster. Copyright © 1993 by Daniel Callahan.

Unless otherwise noted, Scripture quotations are from the New Revised Standard
Version Bible, Copyright 1989 by the Division of Christian Education of the
National Council of the Churches of Christ in the USA. Used by permission.

That noted REB is from the Revised English Bible. Copyright © 1989 Oxford
University Press and Cambridge University Press. Used by permission.

96 97 98 99 00 01 02 03 04 05 — 10 9 8 7 6 5 4 3 2 1
MANUFACTURED IN THE UNITED STATES OF AMERICA

To *Vera Walford of Oxford, England, and to Dr. Ben Wagner of Riverside, Illinois, who graced our lives with wisdom and loving acceptance.*

The theologies we affirm, the philosophies we embrace, the cultural assumptions we presume, serve as a foundation . . . for the attitudes we articulate about life and death, for the medical care we render the dying, for the pastoral care we offer in the face of death, for the rituals we observe when dealing with death and dying, and for the inevitable confrontation with the reality of our own individual mortality.

Rabbi Dr. Byron L. Sherwin

– CONTENTS –

– INTRODUCTION –

The Center for Ethics at Garrett-Evangelical Theological Seminary,* in concert with its associated university, Northwestern, seeks to bring together a unique configuration of parties—seminary, university, congregations, and community groups—both to enable more thoughtful ethical decision making at the personal and parish level, and to influence public policy. With the support of the W. K. Kellogg Foundation, the first project we have undertaken has been that of "Dying Well in the Late Twentieth Century." In this day of Dr. Kevorkian, liver transplants, and scarce yet costly medical resources, every family and faith congregation confronts bewildering decisions as death draws near. How do we meet life's greatest challenge, and how can we do this better?

Perennial wisdom has always held that people die well only when they have lived well. My own pilgrimage as a bioethicist, theologian, and pastor has led me to seek this theoretical ideal within a practical context. For thirty years the new profession that finds theologians and philosophers working in medicine has sought to influence biomedical and legal practice and policy on death and dying by using secular-pluralistic principles such as autonomy, beneficence, and justice. We now realize that ethics must move to the grass roots of our culture. Here at the parochial level, where fundamental beliefs and values are being formed, personal, professional, and public policy decisions are shaped. Here in the congregations, in intimate association of beliefs and commitments, we find ways of living and dying that

*The name of the Center recently has been changed to the Center for Ethics and Values, by action of the Advisory Board, March 28, 1996.

disfigure or transfigure the broader public ethics. As in all realms of ethics today, it is clear that our culture isn't doing very well. Our hope is to create a guide that will help groups in churches and synagogues, and in the society more generally, to grapple with these matters and make fitting resolutions about personal dying, attending one's family and friends in upholding care, and honoring and protecting one another in these momentous and sacred decisions.

This small study book offers readers analysis, proposals, and questions in the hope of stimulating persons, households, congregations, and denominations to come to terms with the crises posed by these new powers we hold at the threshold of death. We also hope it will assist institutions and agencies such as hospitals, nursing homes, hospices, home-care providers, doctors, nurses, courts, and legislators to develop humane and sensitive perspectives and policies on these matters.

A generous pilot project grant from the Kellogg Foundation enabled us to convene experts on the topics and conduct wide-ranging grassroots research at the places where life-and-death decisions are being made. Our findings, presented in this book, show that it is possible to die well in our complicated late twentieth-century world, if certain sensibilities are activated and certain harms avoided.

We call this book a study guide. It is a resource for persons and groups who seek to be morally proactive and prepared to deal with the issues of dying well. Our unfolding story will take us through the social environment, including the law, politics, and economics (chapter 1); through the hard questions faced by those whom we entrust with the ethics of care—physicians and nurses (chapter 2); into theology, the seedbed of our personal, parochial, and public ethics (chapter 3). Then, drawing from the findings of our project, we will look into the actual places where we die (homes, hospitals, hospices, even the streets and other battle zones), asking how communities (chapter 4); clinics (chapter 5); churches and synagogues (chapter 6) are doing in safeguarding our "dying well." We hope this guide will provide a strong course for groups as they ponder these critical issues.

Part One

BASIC ISSUES

Two exaggerated responses to dying reflect the current crisis in belief and value in our society. On the one hand, from fear of threatening death, we pour unending funds into incessant consumption of life-prolonging technology. On the other hand, from fear of pain-filled life, we desperately resort to suicide, assisted or self-inflicted. Less timid persons more commonly face what Dr. Francis Moore, in A Miracle and a Privilege, calls "the terrible situation of fearing death and at the same time wanting it to come as soon as possible."[1]

Such ambivalence raises the question of how we can rejuvenate meaningful personal and social faith and ethics to relieve such anguish. Is it possible to make our life-and-death judgments more appropriate and graceful? How can we better achieve the qualities of good and blessed deaths, which we have defined in this project as

ending one's days in old age, relieved of disabling pain,
surrounded by friends and family,
attended by sensitive caregivers, reconciled with all persons,
in justice and humanity with the world,
at peace with God?

CHAPTER ONE

The Social Setting

*"I feel like a prisoner of forces
beyond my control."*

SOCIETAL PROBLEMS: What forces unique to the late twentieth century act on us today to compound the universal and relentless burden of our mortality? Are these forces—the law, technology, and economics—evil or destructive in themselves, or is their power ambivalent and therefore perhaps subject to some control or management by government, congregations, or individuals? Can the negative side of each be turned to benefit, rather than to harm, dying persons?

A convergence of forces in the social environment—legal salience, technological fascination, and business bias— are among the elements of social culture that shape the experience of dying. A nation that constitutes 5 percent of the global population yet is home to 75 percent of the lawyers in the world can hardly help construing dying, indeed all human problems, more and more in legal terms. This pressure toward moving all human experiences into the litigious and jurispru- dential atmosphere has affected ambivalently the humanity of our dying. Protecting us from abuse and affirming one's rights in dying have been positive contributions of the law. These have been countermanded by the abrogation of freedom and privacy conveyed in the proliferation of mortality law.

The crescendo of technological innovation, combined with the transfer of dying from home to hospital (40% in 1945 to 90% in 1995), also has profoundly altered the conditions of the end-of-life experience for persons and families. Costs, promiscuous medical testing, and economic incentives to keep going or stop—all these add to the disabling confusion (for persons, for households) that often attends the dying process. What are the particulars of these forces? Which laws surrounding mortality affect us most closely? What legal and societal "culture" impinges on our freedoms to choose, or even on our awareness of the kinds of choices we might have? What is our own complicity in the power of technology (medicines, machines, surgical techniques) over our dying? Should economic considerations determine either the kind of care we receive as we lie dying or the quality of our dying?

Law: "Thou shall not kill."

From the first intrusion of divine and human sanctions against killing in divine-right social covenant at the dawn of civilization, suicide and homicide, law and rule, right and punishment have nurtured two convictions in the personal and collective soul: the sacred character of life and the proscription of murder. The biblical dictum found in the celebrative Psalms and the deliberative Job, "The Lord gives and takes away," grounds a spiritual quiescence and a legal resort when people take life and death into their own hands. That God owns human fertility, sterility, morbidity, and mortality discourages autonomous arrogation on our poor part. This communal spirit grounds customs as diverse as coroners' inquests, physicians' qualms about euthanasia, and pastoral consolation.

Present-day law in the realm of death and dying is contoured by two social forces that build upon this archaic impulse. We live in the twilight of Nazi Germany, still morally numb from its genocidal and euthanasic horrors. Alongside this prohibition exists another sociological idea that supports self-life taking. Partly in rejection of Nazi-like totalitarianism and in resonance with older political traditions, we also strongly affirm human rights and self-determination in decision making and prerogatives over one's self and body.

As a society, we have vowed never to recapitulate Mengele's deathly experiments or the gas chambers at Auschwitz, whose prototypes, we remember, were found in the instruments of hospital euthanasia of those considered retarded and demented. One of the research projects at the Center for Ethics looked at attitudes toward accepting and aiding deaths by Holocaust survivors who were themselves now patients or physicians. Dying patients and families who have already once confronted horrific death hold out to extraordinary lengths, employing every measure available to prolong life.[1] Policies such as proscription of PAS (physician assisted suicide) or compulsory routinized CPR (cardiopulmonary resuscitation) reflect that abhorrence of Auschwitz. We save and extend life perhaps to excess.

American medicine, in manifestations ranging from research to treatment innovation, is deeply colored by the vitalistic commitments of persons who reacted to the horror of Nazi disregard for human identity and life. The genius and danger of such commitments is obvious. Rightful remembrance of the Holocaust can ground a blessed reverence for life. It fosters respect for sick and dying persons. But misinterpreting the Holocaust to imply a warriorlike assault on disease, a denial of death's reality, and a relentless pursuit of life-prolongation now become death-prolongation, betrays the very spirit of an ethics of freedom and justice that was sacrificially gained by the martyrs of Buchenwald and Theresiernstadt.

In nations founded in the spirit and ethos of the biblical

tradition, law is grounded in a more primary reality—that of wisdom. This leads us to the sacred translation of dying customs in modern society. In the biblical books of Proverbs or Sirach ethics (the sense of personal and social living that is good, just, and responsible) is promulgated as a basic common-sense or secular wisdom. This steady, nurturing common law, like the wise counsel of a mother or grandmother, grows, flourishes, and sustains a familial and communal life, cultivated by learning, experience, inspiration, and reciprocal expectation among the members of the community.

The secular wisdom portrayed in public policy in refusal of treatment canons, patient self-determination acts, informed consent regulations, and natural-death policies enacted by state legislatures coincides with the reality of limited resources at the personal and familial level and with the recording of "living wills": designating an "agent" to express our will when we may become unable to communicate or be so weak that our wishes are distorted by loved ones and caregivers.

James F. Bresnahan has traced recent developments in social policy and law on dying well. A Jesuit priest and lawyer, Bresnahan has held for many years that the crisis in dying care involves both physician excesses in prolonging the dying process and inordinate desires from persons and families, and the unwillingness to accept death in good faith.[2] The law has swept into this vacuum of what Ivan Illich calls the dangerous conjunction of "rapacious providers and ravenous consumers." The deepest meaning of law challenges this situation. In Torah, the biblical grounding of law in Judeo-Christian society, proverbial wisdom adds elements of character and prudence to casuistic law. In recent social policy, this delicate equipoise of principled sanctity of life and proscription of murder, and the avoidance of experiencing and inflicting suffering, is maintained. We have achieved a kind of prudential wisdom where rule is tailored to circumstance.

Bresnahan locates a prudential ethos that underlies the

jurisprudential culture in several social movements, the first
of which was the awareness of the staging progression of
death and dying in the work of Elisabeth Kübler-Ross. This
sequencing of experience from resistance to acquiescence
established dying once again as a benign and natural process. The hospice movement begun by Dr. Cicely Saunders
in England has afforded profound humanization of the
dying process, with its emphasis on complete pain relief
without absurd bickering about terminal addiction, patient
self-titration and administration of drugs, but above all,
intimate involvement of caregivers, families, and friends in
an informal atmosphere of care and support, and the addition of psychological and spiritual support as aspects of
good palliative and medical care. To these developments I
would add the social and medical acknowledgment of
patients' rights to forgo treatment even when such would
prolong their living; the validation of "living wills" as
appropriate and binding written or vocal indications of a
person's wish at the stage of dying; and the tentative acceptance of double-effect euthanasia, in cases where continued
analgesic (morphine) relief of suffering and offering of comfort might foreshorten the dying process.

These dimensions of value have been established slowly
but firmly in the law and communal wisdom and have
become embodied in the processes of medical care.

Legal History

The emergence of this value structure in contemporary
America resulted from two forces in our social history.
Modern history has taught us an ethical wisdom wherein we
reject totalitarian collectivism and libertarian individualism.
This is part of the deeper human assertion of the limited
and conditioned virtue of the values of *égalité* and *hierarché*,
and responsible freedom in service within community. We

have settled now on a value matrix that might be called a person-respecting communalism, or a communally toned individualism.

As noted earlier, we recently have emerged from a period of totalitarian history that had as its cornerstone an active ideology of ethnic cleansing, eugenics, and euthanasia. The "common good" and "collective health" were thought to be served by expressing Darwinian selection in the realm of health-and-life, birth-and-death decisions. The era began with sterilization policy in certain states of America, which developed into the Nazi eugenic policy. In Germany in the 1920s and 1930s, euthanasia policy eased those considered retarded, demented, and no longer productive into engineered deaths. This utopian totalitarianism was grounded in earlier racist, hygienic, and biologic theories that believed it noble to eliminate the weak, aged, injured, and constitutionally disabled for the sake of the vitality of the social organism. "Too many mouths to feed." That view was as old as Plato and the Renaissance utopias. It is good, such collectivist programs felt, to move the decrepit along, lest the burden of care overwhelm the resources of the society.

This ethic is still with us. In recent years, for example, "right-to-die" initiatives such as the Patient Self-Determination Act (PSDA) have been appended to budget and expenditure legislation. Whether it be in early twentieth-century Germany or late twentieth-century America, nationalist and socialist impulses often blend mischievously into health policy. Among conservatives, abortion is often discountenanced, as it was with the Nazis. General prolongevist policy is often combined with selective diminution of health care services for minorities and the poor. We end up with strange inconsistencies such as we have in late twentieth-century American cities (and rural areas), where the terminal care treatments are exotic and life experiences are rich in the rural areas, while morbidity (e.g., poor cancer treatment) and premature mortality abound just down the highway in the adjacent urban area. One mitigating factor in this unjust communalist ethic and its guided health system is the advanced tertiary university hospital, often situated in the indigent inner city. Here the sick poor, wounded by a lifetime of societal neglect, especially in education, housing, and employment, now die early (on the average 10 years earlier than their white suburban counterparts) under sophisticated intensive care. Advanced coronary, geriatric, and neonatal intensive-care units populated by poor blacks and other minorities is one of the grotesque symptoms of social pathology in the body of our ethically diseased community.

We have surveyed the legal and cultural fabric of our society, showing that the political and civil soil in which death-and-dying decisions must be made is rich and capable of different kinds of growth. This ground retains the historic normative commitment to honor and sustain life, and not to kill. It especially surrounds with taboo and guilt/ remorse rituals those who in conscience find it necessary to accept, even hasten death in the elderly, seriously impaired newborns, embryos, and fetuses. This keeps tragic necessity from becoming evil. Profound respect for and protection of living beings is a prerequisite for stable and creative societies. Law and social custom embody this ethic.

Technology: "Is new necessarily better?"

The social environment also impinges on our dying through biomedical technology. Three areas of technology that change the ways we die are medicines, machines, and surgical techniques. While there should be freedom for caregivers to use or not use these technologies and freedom for patients to call or not call for them, their very presence tends to encourage their use. This is especially true in an adversarial and acquisitive society. Providers fear lawsuits if

they don't do everything. Vested interests want to compound the hospital bill as much as possible.

In the sequel to our current project, the Center for Ethics
will explore the issues that arise at the intersection of medical
research, treatment, and health-care delivery. Surprisingly, very
little attention has been given to the question of how new
developments in research change treatments that are offered
and how these in turn modify the way health care is delivered.
Legally and morally, and of course medically, we are obliged to
offer patients "state of the art" care for their condition. This
ethical requirement is difficult to fulfill when we realize that
the "art" is always advancing. Given our penchant for innovation for innovation's sake and the "market-drivenness" of
biotechnology, we can never know if new is necessarily good.

Medicines can prolong living in one disease state, make the
morbidity of the disease (pain, injury) more bearable, or rem-
edy the condition by making room for something else to afflict
us. Patients or caregivers of course do not raise these kinds of
speculations. When distress occurs, we simply and carefully
seek something to relieve it. The reward system for physicians
(praise, payment, and continuing clientele) opts for short-term
relief rather than freedom from longer-range crisis. We request
and treat the staph infection rather than pondering the implication of host resistance. We consent to the Whipple procedure and secondary chemotherapy for the malignancy at the
head of the pancreas and allay our immediate fears and hopes.
In this immediate response, we set aside for now the question
of what new terminal condition and course of dying we have
set ourselves up for. At best, medicines resonate with and aid
the body's self-healing, and residual side effects are successfully
absorbed and overcome by the organism.

Machines such as respirators, dialyzers, and the like carry
us through physiological crises. They also permanently
appendage our body by replicating a failed function. I still
remember early in my clinical career meeting a young man,

his heart destroyed by cardiomyopathy, living and functioning by a machine installed on the front of his chest. The machine, called AVAD (artificial ventricular assist device), pumped blood through the deprived body.

The resident took me aside and said, "The man is already dead except for the machine. Later today, as his other organs fail, we will disconnect him, and he'll be gone." Surgery similarly reroutes the course of our lives, spares us from impending morbidity (e.g., acute abdomen) for some other morbidity, and thus mortality, causally or incidentally related to that intervention.

Biotechnology is a gift of God and a boon to human fulfillment. Think of the polio vaccine, penicillin, the respirator, or kidney transplantation. When used to serve the life trajectory or as life-saving procedures, these and all the preventions and interventions that they represent are good. When they disrupt the dying trajectory, or when they stabilize failing life in a debilitated state, their efficacy is questionable. When they damage or foreshorten life or fashion greater injustice and iniquity among peoples, their moral ambivalence is accentuated. Intentionally good efforts can become evil. Therefore, acute ethical discernment becomes crucial.

Economics: "Do we have too many mouths to feed? Should some of us move over to make room for younger folk?"

The economic environment also determines decisions we must make as we face death. Today in the United States, it is not uncommon to spend $50,000 or $100,000 on medical care in the last days and weeks of our lives. The concern here is obvious. We may be pouring an intolerable portion of our own personal, family, and public resources into death and dying. Right now we are so affluent that the terror of this allocation does not strike us.

When your estate is worth one-half million dollars, a $100,000 expense at life's end can be absorbed. But what if your net worth is $2,000? What if you die with a negative "net-worth sheet"? Social Security pays $250 for a funeral —that doesn't help much. For increasingly larger numbers of people, the costs of health-care insurance and, if uninsured or co-insured, out-of-pocket costs for health care are becoming prohibitive. Will health-care costs level off at 14 percent of GNP, or will they rapidly accelerate or decelerate? Social and ethical judgments of enormous import confront us.

At the micro level, people also must make economic choices when they die. To tend the *ecos*, the house we live in, is at the root not only of ecumenical but also of ecological and economic choices. Shall I use the $100,000 I have saved to send my daughter to college or undergo a program of treatments for pancreatic carcinoma? A tough choice, given the questionable value of either course of action. Each may work and the world may be bettered as a result. Each may fail. The economic question is a two-edged sword: Some people today strive to prolong life at any cost. This can become the idolatry of vitality. Some people feel it is better to stop striving and give up. This can be the idolatry of mortality. Home care (economic) decisions have joined the ultimate (theological) questions of our time.

At a rudimentary naturalistic level, death-care ethics are ecological and economic considerations. All lives must pass on and yield vitality and ascendancy to a new generation. "There is a time to be born and a time to die" recites the generic justice of social equilibrium. This reality counterbalances vitalistic and prolongevist excesses, constantly chides those who perpetuate suffering in the name of life prolongation, and economically, albeit subconsciously, maintains proportion in the birth-death ratio of a society.

CHAPTER TWO

The Medical Setting

"What does it mean, finally, to 'do no harm'? How can I allow this patient to suffer endlessly and mercilessly?"

Plagued by multiple burdens of long years of grueling and expensive medical training, heavy caseloads, and rapidly escalating amounts of available information, the doctor of the late twentieth century may find that he or she is not "the great physician" or a pastor or a healer, but merely a body manager, a technician. What are the dimensions of the physician's practice? How might the tradition(s) within which a physician practices affect his or her openness to change, particularly in the area of dying? Could it be said that personal anguish at patient misery or at the impotence of the caregiver to give care—time, attention, or what both patient and doctor ardently desire, health—might push a physician toward the safety of time-honored conservatism and away from active engagement with ethical questions or consideration of alternative expressions of care of dying patients?

Medicine in our day has traversed an enormous and tangled landscape. In honoring the gift of life and health, it has affirmed (to excess) the virtue of vitality. In honoring the stricture against inflicting or perpetuating suffering, it has sometimes too readily extolled merciful release from life. The evolving ethos of medicine is entering a new phase in our present time. Health professionals today are making more nuanced judgments about when to serve living and when to honor dying.

Society licenses doctors and thereby authorizes the profession's claim of competence and the society's need for help. In this act of legalizing some and criminalizing others, physicians are given a significant trust over our living and dying. Out of this sociocultural commitment to the propagating, perpetuating, and processing of living beings, society designates the healing professions as callings entrusted with authority to superintend these processes. The moral/covenantal/contractual legacy of the medical profession within the ethics of terminal care constitutes another essential component of the setting wherein dying decisions must be made and values confronted. Let us set in place this next piece of the puzzle, looking first at the historical ethics of physicians about human dying and then at some reexamination and reappropriation of those values.

The moral roots of the Western medical professions are Hellenic and Hebraic-Christian. Both traditions proscribe medical killing, euthanasia, and usually aid-in-dying, except when this is entailed in the relief of suffering. The Hippocratic oath arises out of fifth-century BCE Greek ethics in the rationalistic and naturalistic spirit of that commitment. The oath warns physicians against ending life *in utero* or *in vivo*. The yet unborn and the presently alive are to be honored. This Hippocratic value exudes a holiness (Pythagorean) dimension and stands in conflict with the infanticidal and gerematricidal tendencies of the Hellenistic culture.

In the Bible, as it summarizes the Judean and Jesus stories in the Hebrew Testament and the Christian Testament (with the salvation history these teachings give to the world), the weak, poor, and vulnerable are extolled and the dying are dignified. This new estimate ("Jerusalem") starkly contrasts with the dark side of the Hellenic and more general pagan ethos ("Athens"), which honored body-mind-beauty and strength, discarded imperiled children, and abandoned the dying.

The more recent physician ethic on care of the dying is decisively influenced by revulsion to the Nazi euthanasia practice and the right-to-life tendencies of the conservative political and religious agenda of recent decades. When compounded by fear of litigation and the fear of failure and death, this general conservative inclination tends to continue diagnostic and therapeutic interventions while patients are dying. Just as heroism in the patient is honored by words such as "Joe was a fighter to the end," physician heroics extol, "Dr. Jones did everything he possibly could."

In the United States, from the mid-twentieth century on, the prevailing professional ethic of medicine has become more conservative than the longer tradition of "letting go." In the late twentieth century, ethics policy on abortion has been shaped by a defensive and embattled Catholic posture that opposes abortion. The longer moral view of the medical profession toward dying has been suppressed and the right-to-life position extended to embrace euthanasia and end-of-life decisions. A conservative right-to-life tendency in ethics, combined with a burgeoning life-prolonging technology and a business interest in using it, has wreaked human havoc, especially when the transition from life to death is relocated from homes to anonymous, impersonal hospitals, and otherwise sensible people make senseless decisions.

In recent years the medical professions, especially nursing, finding with the Apostle that "the good they would do, they cannot," have come to terms with these moral contradictions. An ethic of "all-systems-go" has slowly yielded to an ethic that

- invites patient participation in decisions;
- does not uncritically push on unless it is indicated and all agree;
- discerns when further interventions are futile;
- willingly forgoes unnecessary tests and treatments;
- withdraws life-sustaining supports when indicated and requested;
- offers pain relief even when it shortens the dying process;
- cautiously begins discussion, privately and publicly, about aid-in-dying.

One physician who helped our project explore this unfolding aspect of "dying well" was Timothy Quill. Dr. Quill, an internist in New York State, is widely known and respected for his sensitive struggling with these issues and for his provocative report in the March 7, 1991, issue of the *New England Journal of Medicine* on his patient Diane.[1] Diane was a young woman stricken, as are so many young men and women today, with a probably incurable malignancy. She fought, she acceded, she asked for help to end her suffering and spare herself and her supporters final indignity.

In the mid-1990s, several physicians have sought to develop ethical grounds to undergird this course of action. We will review Quill's position, along with similar positions by Howard Brody, a family physician in Michigan, and Harvard surgeon Francis D. Moore. Each of these physicians seeks to ground a selective aid-in-dying care-plan in the deepest traditions of humane and ethical medical care. Our point in reviewing the arguments of these important caregivers is not to justify a position of hastening death, but to discuss through their unfolding arguments the elements of enlightened and compassionate terminal care.[2] Throughout, we hold in tandem the perspective of Dr. Jan van Eys, who reminds us that "there is a dark side to mercy. The relationship between those who receive mercy and those who mete out mercy is uneven. The merciful are dominant over the mercy-needful." He continues: "[Euthanasia and assisted suicide] may be something a physician feels compelled to do . . . [but] physicians who want to ease the passage of a suffering patient actively must do so with profound humility. They must reject the notion that they are doing an act of mercy. If they do not, the very act of euthanasia is apt to generate self-justification. . . . As long as the act of euthanasia is seen as an act of mercy, implicit empowerment occurs. . . . It is the *physician* [not the patient] who is given the power to decide how life will end."[3]

Quill: "Conversation"

"This is a book of wisdom and compassion," reviews Yale surgeon Sherwin Nuland, himself the author of a similarly magnificent study, *How We Die.*[4] Diane decided not to undergo chemotherapy for her acute myelomonocytic leukemia. She had a 25 percent chance for a long-term cure but decided against it. She also asked Dr. Quill to provide a lethal prescription of barbituates. He did. Those are the raw facts. The interstitial story is one of unwavering and struggle, of resolute conviction and severe doubt, of extraordinary sympathy and kindness. Diane's support community was there for her, but in the end she chose, and they allowed her, to die alone. This fact continues to trouble Dr. Quill: "I make a solemn promise to my dying patients that I will not abandon them, no matter where their illness may take them."[5]

What are the elements of "wisdom and compassion" that prompted Dr. Quill to take a controversial position and assist Diane in achieving death in her own way? First, he talked with her. He spent many hours in candid sharing. He contended for his perspective on things, though with evident willingness to suspend his views in favor of hers. He communicated respect for her authority.

This commitment to conversation may sound routine, but in fact, it is quite extraordinary. Doctors rarely have time for intensive engagement and more rarely have the security to allow patients their free thought and will. "I know best," or "You couldn't possibly understand" has traditionally been the paternalistic evasion of genuine mutuality in decision making. In partnering one who is approaching death, a delicate balance is required. The doctor must be knowledgeable, resolute, committed, and engaged. The vulnerability, fear, and passivity of the patient are often heightened at this threshold of life. But physicians must not be overbearing. The patient must be allowed to die her own death, orchestrating the process to the extent that she is willing and able.

Another feature of Dr. Quill's care was companionship. Throughout the ordeal, the doctor should be the patient's friend. This is especially necessary as death nears. The patient needs to know that his/her doctor is there for him/her, will not be bothered by calls or queries, will not grow impatient or bored when there is nothing left to "try" or "do," and will not slowly move away, become too busy, or take leave. The reward systems of medicine do not encourage companionship. Ego-rewards come from doing something that works or helps, not just "being there." Remunerative systems generally do not pay for in-depth consultation or consolation. Especially in recent years, a physician must show concrete interventions to impress the reimbursers.

Brody: "Integrity"

In addition to Quill and Christine Cassel of the University of Chicago, another physician who has written most eloquently about this quality of terminal care is Howard Brody. I remember when Howard Brody was a medical student. He was preparing a manual on ethics for physicians-in-training and visited Joe Fletcher and me when we were working together in the Texas Medical Center in Houston. Brody has developed his position in two salient essays.[6] The essence of his moral argument is that physicians have taken on a professional role and identity by virtue of their relationships with patients. Using both secular and religious concepts of contract and covenant, Brody holds that a special trust is assumed when cultivated in the office of the physician. The essence of this ethical responsibility Brody calls "integrity."

Integrity can be viewed as a jewel with many facets. It means that a life is lived out in terms of a coherent and meaningful narrative. The ethical life must be integral and whole. One cannot believe one thing and do another. One cannot behave one way at one moment and the opposite at some other moment. Integrity means to be reliable, trustworthy. Jews call this life *shalom*. The life of integrity involves obedience to one's conscience. One cannot be expected to violate one's conscience. In terms of "killing" or "helping to die," we feel the immediate force of this axiom with reference to abortion and euthanasia. The opposite of conscientious integrity is adaptive expediency. Here we become the person and perform the action that is expected of us. "I was only following orders," pleaded the Nazi doctors at Nuremberg.

Brody is broaching philosophically what Quill and Cassel approach ontologically as the duty of "nonabandonment."[7] The principle of nonabandonment, staked out in diametric opposition to the Hippocratic virtue of abandoning the dying patient, contends that a caring, continuous contact must be maintained with the terminal patient. Staying true and present to the end will fashion a fidelity that often will disclose the imperatives of mercy. Drawing on strands of conviction from casuistic, feminist, and narrative ethics, their proposal blends duty and principle, justice and mercy, philosophy and theology into a more theistically and humanistically adequate morality.

Before we leave medical perspectives on our theme, the writings of two surgeons, Sherwin Nuland and Francis Moore, deserve special mention, not only for their erudition but for the powerful realism of the view they offer. Perhaps the most widely read book on our subject in recent years is Nuland's *How We Die*. By virtue of his craft, the surgeon is offered an intimate window into the brutal malignancy, the mechanical failure, the seething and seeping infection, the morbid and mortal wound of the body. The realism of this surgical perspective has contributed to the emerging ethos that we are sketching. Nuland elaborates this story by describing death from cancer, heart disease, and AIDS, among other conditions. We will summarize his thought in the next section on theological perspectives.

Reflecting on the years of his own practice, Francis Moore recalls a good day, the intrusion of a new and ominous day, and the slight hint on the horizon of a sensible return:

> Going back to my internship days, I can remember many patients in pain, sometimes in coma or delirious, with late, hopeless cancer. For many of them we wrote an order for heavy medication to be given regularly by the nurses. We were assisting with a softer exit from this world. This was not talked about openly. It was essential, not controversial. . . .
>
> With such measures as assisted respiration, assisted heart-beat, and an artificial kidney, many patients who want surcease from life now are being kept alive, either by machines or by the machinations of physicians or family. They have managed to survive too far into the progress of disease by dint of their own efforts, better hygiene, and nutrition. While doctors may not have been guilty of keeping them here, they need guidance on helping them leave.[8]

When we turn to our empirical observations of clinical care toward the goal of dying well, we will see that a delicate balance is now being sought between fighting for life and letting go in due season. Societal resources and personal wishes are given primacy within the context of caregiver professional ethics and transcendent spiritual values.[9] We now turn to the latter set of considerations as we survey the shifting theological terrain that ultimately grounds the economic, legal, technical, and medical matters of dying well. We have held throughout our project the thesis that spiritual immaturity will contort these practical decisions into bizarre and grotesque forms, while spiritual wisdom will undergird the benign, even blessed, *ars moriendi*—the art of dying.

CHAPTER THREE

The Theological Setting

"If I have faith, why am I so frightened of death?" "I will never understand how God could have allowed Mother to suffer for so many years."

"Life is the destiny you are bound to refuse until you have consented to die."[1]

Aware of the societal dimensions and dementias that frame but also punctuate our lives, instructed and yet terrified by the medical realities on which we must depend, we remain questing, feeling, sorrowing, or rejoicing creatures. We will now review three theologies of dying and death, theologies that always have been with human persons since we first emerged as "homo religiosis." Each theology retains some element required by human honesty to the experience of dying and death. Each retains some element of response to that facinans tremendum, that mystery we find in and beyond death. In the face of death, there is a theology of unreality, of brutality, and of magnanimity. In a fascinating way, the history of religion and the humanities, and the history of science and medicine itself play out these underlying theologies. Each theology contains some sense of accountability about death and some notion of appropriate response to death. Each theology therefore expresses and gives shape to a basic ethical and practical approach as we live out our lives in the world.

In examining Theologies A and B, we must ask ourselves, how is each—"death as friend," "death as enemy"—expressed in our society? What are the biblical foundations of a theology of death that resists death in the name of God and life, yet accepts death trusting in God's faithfulness and resurrection power over death? How do we live out that theology in our dying? Finally, in the pastoral care of the congregation, how do we honor and affirm appropriate fear of and resistance to death along with appropriate acceptance?

To develop the theological background of our theme of "Dying Well," I will trace the history and present ramifications of each of these theologies of death. I will argue that the third *modus moriendi*, magnanimity (to borrow a phrase from Sir William Osler), will be most true to the data of empirical and transcendental experience and most conducive to a humane and spiritual response to human dying.

Let me begin with an experience from my own clinical work. Laurie was as bubbly and vivacious a fourteen-year-old as you'd ever find. Her life changed forever when she found a blemish on her cheek, in the same spot where her mother had had a malignant lesion successfully removed some years before. She came to M. D. Anderson Cancer Center in Houston. The transitional cell carcinoma had invaded the head and neck, and manifold surgeries, chemo, and radiation therapies followed. She became the first human being in history to be placed on 14 grams of methotrexate—a cytotoxic assault that eventually combined with the disease to kill her. We worked out a covenant to learn with one another about living and dying in the good world of God.

The *dramatis personae* around her talked and lived out these three theologies of death that are common to Protestant, Roman Catholic, and Jewish faiths, and indeed appear in some form in all the great faiths.[2] In Laurie's case, the Roman Catholic co-parishioners and priest who visited her when she returned to the small town in Missouri distracted her from her disease to the other reality of God and Jesus. Like contemporary Gnostics or Christian Scientists, they sought to transport her to the realm of spirit, where peace, joy, and life prevailed. Doctors, pioneering chemical investigations, knew the brutal force of malignancy and death, and pulled out all the weapons to attack the enemy.

Laurie lived out that delicate equipoise of resistance and resignation, of aggressive hope and acquiescence—the living theology we call magnanimity. I will quote throughout this chapter from a diary she gave me when we last met before her death some seventeen years ago:

> One thing that helped me with the pain and not to complain was thinking about all the pain the Lord went through. It couldn't be one half the pain he went through all his life. He had so much criticism the same as some of us. He said if you can take this cup away from me do it (I said that too; either end this now or just get rid of it). He always had to fight for people even to understand who He really was. You really have to learn to send different messages to your brain besides pain. At first that takes lots of effort, but if you put forth that effort early it becomes easier later.

This Jesus picture and the incarnational condition of what Christ means in life and death is as vivid with Laurie as it is in the new studies of the historical Jesus by J. D. Crossan and E. P. Saunders.[3] Dealing with the terror of pain and consequent self-pity, Laurie continues:

> It was also important not to draw back and feel sorry for myself. There's always somebody who's worse off than you. That might be kind of hard to imagine, but it's true. I can have cancer and get it over with. Some people suffer for years and years, some people are born retarded and all their life are shunned and shoved back by society, never being brought forward. Whenever I started to feel sorry for myself, I had a hell of a time coming back and being part of things.

This was an amazing social and theological understanding of her plight. Laurie's pilgrimage with her ethically eclectic entourage of caregivers sets the stage for our analysis.

Theology A: "Death as Friend"

Theology A is the theology of death's unreality or, put another way, death's fundamental impotence. This is the theology of Platonism and Gnosticism. It is the exaltation enthusiasm confronted by the Apostle Paul in 1 Corinthians 15. It is found in certain senses of Nirvana—assorted schools of Buddhism, or Jihad warriors in Iranian Islam who gleefully awaited instant transition to Paradise when they fell on the Iraqi frontier. It is found in some strands of Hinduism and Christian Science. It is promulgated by near-death analysis and life-after-life astronauts, from Elisabeth Kübler-Ross to Raymond Moody and Shirley MacLaine. This theology has certain perennial features. Death is either a figment of finitude that is distorted material imagination, or it becomes a flash point of transfer to another reality. The theology often accompanies highly spiritualist and idealist metaphysics and worldviews. It correlates with certain psychic personality and characterology conditions, not necessarily pathologic. If Marx, Freud, Durkheim, Feuerbach, and to some extent Nietzsche are to be followed, it may correlate with certain kinds of sociogenic desperation and fantasy. It may be related to militias and suicidal cultism.

Now if you are starting to cordon off a whole cadre of lunatics and heretics as the death deniers, let us draw back to reality. This theology is also commonplace. We all often treat death as if it hadn't happened. Someone has died. You wake up the next morning, and the same waitress throws the scrambled eggs at the same restaurant, and the same newsboy peddles papers as if nothing had happened. This is not the simple denial of busy, nonpensive, exuberant people. We all seem to get on with business as usual, as if death were unreal. As Rabbi Byron Sherwin has commented, "We regularly use euphemisms to avoid death . . . the deceased is referred to as the 'departed' . . . the grave is called a 'resting place.' "[4] Most people do show amazing resilience in the face of death, grief, and bereavement. We have an uncanny ability to get up the next day and get on with life as if death didn't happen. I interpret this as the normal human coping mechanism of denial, tinged with illusions born in the biology and psychology of hope.

What are the virtues and vices of Theology A? It surely is a strength that this theology recognizes that this life is not all there is. It acknowledges the reality of God supervening the reality of this world. It recognizes the contingency of space, time, and matter, and the reality of eternity. With Augustine and Luther, it trusts that all tribulation flows from the benevolent will of God.

The danger of Theology A is manifold. As a teenager conscripted into Hitler's army at the incendiary end of the war, Jürgen Moltmann realized that this generation of lost and disillusioned youth craved and welcomed death. They threw themselves into the mouth of the cannon and looked with glee on the fire storms over Dresden and Hamburg. Why? Because they hated themselves, they despised their wretched lives. The flaw in Theology A that is common to all dualism is the deprecation of life and the body. Our colleague, church historian Dr.

Dennis Groh, feels that it took the Christian sect of Jews until the fifth century to overcome Hellenism, for the soul and body again to become friends. There may come a point at which we do despise the flesh, when malignant or infectious invasions, proliferate occupations, and corruptions of the body lead us to wish to slough off this mortal coil. In weariness, we then see the leaden interaction that is our body, as the children with cancer show in their drawings—butterflies encased in cocoons or birds confined in cages, and we desire release.

Theology A may prompt death acceptance or death wish. A salutary impulse, it becomes destructive in exaggeration. Theology A also makes it easier to kill another. The conquistadors baptized the babies of aboriginal Indian tribes, then smashed their heads on the rocks. They had been translated to heaven. Better to die now than to endure this harsh and tempting world. I wonder if genocidal invasions in Bosnia are blessed by the priests. Genocide, homicide, suicide, even ecocide almost seem to require Theology A, *contemptus vivendi.* Believing and living Theology A involves some disdain for one's own body. There is something cold-hearted about dispatching oneself or another to the realm of death.

Bastille Day at Maison Vaux usually means a French film. Last year it was *Un Coeur en Hiver (A Heart in Winter).* Stephen, the consummate violin builder and repairer, is played by Daniel Auteuil, who will be remembered as the aroused yet muted mountain boy in *Jean de Florette* and *Manon of the Spring.* In *A Heart in Winter,* he plays a kind of inversion of a Wesley character whose heart is strangely cooled. He is remembered by his siblings as devious as a child. His jealousy is stirred when his business partner's affection is drawn to a lovely virtuoso, Camille. His own affection is then drawn to her in what proves to be a destructive lure. He invites her love but then rejects it. In tortuous Pauline soul crisis in which he can't do his will and does his antiwill, his muted heart is deaf and dumb. In the end, Camille also dies within. In a successful but loveless career, she plays Ravel's sonatas with technical precision but lacking inspiration. In a poignant scene in this day of Dr. Kevorkian—a scene which might point to some of the virtue of this theology—Stephen (cold heart) alone among the circle of close friends is able to deliver the *coup de grace*, the lethal injection to the suffering old friend (played by Yves Montand). The old friend had tried to teach Stephen through life the grace of house-holding care and family love. The scene recalls that Passover upper room, where a firebrand called Judas is told by his Rabbi: "Do quickly what you are going to do" (John 13:27). The apocalyptic and eschatological rendition of reality which, if not the Jesus consciousness, is the apostolic consciousness, measured life and death against eternity. In a positive sense, it defies the vitalistic and mechanistic manias of an age like ours. Karl Rahner, in his *Theology of Death*, says that we are to die like Jesus, steadfastly, with eyes fixed on Jerusalem, with courage, heartily.

> Those who find their life will lose it, and those who lose their life for my sake will find it. (Matthew 10:39)

But we must pause for a moment when we mention the death of Jesus.

Theology B: "Death as Enemy"

Oscar Cullmann has given us a memorable essay comparing the death of Socrates and the death of Jesus, as reported by Plato and the synoptic evangelists. The death of Socrates is serene and confident. The outer garment of the body will pass away, but Socrates will live on by virtue of the eternal bearing and belonging of the soul, and the ethical justice of his life. One goes home in peace and composure—death is beautiful.

Jesus dies differently. In the garden he trembles and is distressed—"I am deeply grieved, even to death." This is not divine bliss or automatic translation to paradise. It is dreadful. "Let this cup pass from me." "My God, why have you forsaken me?" Death, for Jesus, is the enemy of God. It entails desolation and being utterly forsaken. Despite the undergirding Hebraic truth that God kills and enlivens, Jesus' anguished death emphasizes that other Semitic strain that God is life, life's creator and sustainer. Death severs us from God. To summarize, Cullmann writes:

> If we want to understand the Christian faith in the resurrection, we must completely disregard the Greek thought that the material, the bodily, the corporeal is bad and must be destroyed, so that the death of the body would not be in any sense a destruction of the true life. For Christian and Jewish thinking, the death of the body is also destruction of God-created life. The distinction is made—even the life of our body is true life. Therefore, it is death and not the body which must be conquered by the resurrection.[5]

In this mood we celebrate. Even the brutal and disfiguring assaults of breast or facial cancer is fathomed in the divine benediction of life. Jesus illuminated death as the harsh, brutal reality that it is. While John Cobb goes too far (in his volume on the *Liberation of Life*) in suggesting that life is God, it is true that God is life.

There is a horrible brutality to death in Theology B. In a refreshingly candid and realistic book, after one has had enough of the "death is so nice" theology, Yale surgeon Sherwin Nuland has written *How We Die: Reflections on Life's Final Chapter.* Here we have not death as the fantastic voyage, or even the more innocuous "Death is a part of life." As Nuland describes six modern modes of dying, we see death as an intruder, a rude usurper who consumes all our powers of endurance, grace, and dignity, a "looming terror and looming temptation" which we attempt to mute and beat with all the powers of resistance and evasion. Medicine itself now joins battle in John Donne's "Death's Duel."

Nuland describes death from heart failure and cancer, AIDS and Alzheimer's, and when disease deaths are finally displaced by inflicted deaths, he describes the mortality of accidents and violence. Surgeons are usually untroubled by reflection and meaning. They are bench workers and crafts-men. They also allow our rage to come out. Nuland describes an encounter with one patient, a forty-year-old attorney on whom he had operated for breast cancer. Why is it, I often wonder, that the ligatures of life-giving become those of death-dealing—the sexual (endocrinal) axes—breast, cervix, endometrium, ovarian, prostate, testes? Was this why Hebraic holiness theology held that purity required cleanliness from life and death vitalities—semen, menstruation, cadavers?

The young woman asked Nuland for a talk after a follow-up visit gave her the good news that she was still clear. She then began to describe, as Laurie did, the identical disease in her mother, who had just died in another way. "My mother died in agony," she said, "and no matter how hard the doctors tried, they couldn't make things easy for her." She continued, betraying her naïveté in Theology A: "It was nothing like the peaceful end I expected. I thought it would be spiritual, that we would talk about her life, about the two of us together. But it never happened. There was too much pain, too much Demerol." And then in one outburst of tearful rage, she said, "Dr. Nuland, there was no dignity to my mother's death!" We recall one-time Garrett professor Paul Ramsey's moving essay, "The Indignity of Death with Dignity." The expecta-tion of a good death, a serene death, as the deserving of the righteous—indeed, the connection of death with goodness or evil—still haunts us. This is a theme we will return to when we look at 1 Corinthians 15 and Romans 5, the classic texts of "thanatol-theology" and the real charter of death's brutality.

Death is the wages of sin; death is the last enemy. Disease, not death, says Nuland, is the enemy. "Death is the surcease that comes when the exhausting battle has been lost" (p. 10). Heart disease and ultimate failure, writes Nuland, is an "unforgiving sickness, like so many other causes of death, is a

progressive continuum whose ultimate role in our planet's
ecology is the quenching of human life" (p. 19). Taking issue
with Cullmann and joining with Elisabeth Kübler-Ross,
Nuland might argue that death is an essential "part of life."

But in the sober descriptive sections of this moving book,
it sounds like the Bible in its realism. Death is brutal because
of the converging burden of sin and disease. Nuland
describes the helpless doctor watching the cardiac demise of
Horace Giddens in Lillian Hellman's play *Little Jones:*

> Horace Giddens died on a rainy afternoon. . . . Although
> present, I was unable to lift a finger to help him. I could do
> nothing but sit by as his wife verbally abused him, until he
> suddenly threw his hand up to his throat, as though gesturing
> toward the brutal pathway of his radiating angina. His pallor
> suddenly increasing, he began to gasp, then shakily groped
> for the solution of nitroglycerin that lay on a coffee table in
> front of the wheelchair in which he sat. He managed only to
> get his fingers around it, but it fell from his trembling hand
> to the floor and shattered, spilling the precious medicine that
> might have widened his coronary arteries just enough to save
> him. Panic-stricken and breaking out into a cold sweat, he
> begged Regina [his wife] to find the maid, who knew where
> his reserve bottle was kept. She didn't move. Increasingly
> agitated, he tried to shout, but the only sound to come out of
> his mouth was a hoarse whisper, too small to be heard out-
> side the room. The look on his face was heart-rending to see,
> as he realized the futility of his strangled efforts.
>
> I felt impelled to rush to Gidden's assistance but some-
> thing held me rooted to my chair. I didn't do a thing, and
> neither did anyone else. He made a sudden furious spring
> from his wheelchair to the stairs, taking the first few steps
> like a desperate runner trying with his last iota of energy to
> reach safety. On the fourth step, he slipped, gasped hungrily
> for air, seized the railing, and, in one great exhausted effort
> of grimacing finality, reached the landing on his knees.
> Frozen in my place, I gazed up the stairs at him and saw his

legs give way. Everyone in that room heard the crumpling sound of his body falling forward, just out of view.

Giddens was still alive, but barely. Regina, with the calm dispatch of an experienced assassin, called out to two of the servants to carry him into his room. The family physician was summoned. Within a few minutes, and long before the doctor arrived, his stricken patient was dead. (pp. 33-4)

Joseph of Arimathea was there when they took him down. The stricken patient was dead. After all the fluff and marshmallow, the only religious texts I find to be equally as candid as Nuland, and thereby liberating, are 1 Corinthians 15 and Romans 5. We annually traverse them in the Easter litany, unless we've fled away to crocuses, spring, and Easter parades:

1 Corinthians	For since death came through a human being, the resurrection of the dead has also come through a human being; for as all die in Adam, so all will be made alive in Christ. . . . For he must reign until he has put all his enemies under his feet. The last enemy to be destroyed is death. (15:21-22, 25-26)
Romans	For while we were still weak, at the right time Christ died for the ungodly. Indeed, rarely will anyone die for a righteous person. . . . But God proves his love for us in that while we still were sinners, Christ died for us. . . . Therefore, just as sin came into the world through one man, and death came through sin . . . but where sin increased, grace abounded all the more. (5:6-7*a*, 8, 12*a*, 20*b*)

In these texts, Paul is struggling against both Theology A and Theology B. In both Corinth and Rome, there were dreamers who said that there was no death, and deniers who said that there was no resurrection. Paul responds:

The wages of sin is death. . . . Christ died for our sins . . .
and was buried. . . . How can some of you say there is no
resurrection? . . . If Christ has not been raised . . . you are still
in your sins. (Romans 6:23*a;* 1 Corinthians 15:3-4, 12, 17)

Paul's conclusion against the exaltation enthusiasts, who
fashioned a mystification of death, and the dreary death-
mongers who called folks back to the tables of hedonic Epicureanism, was a majestically realistic hope—what in our
last section we will call *magnanimity.*

Christ has overcome sin, yes, but the residue of death
remains. The last enemy to be defeated in the cosmic history of God will be death. Resurrection is an exceptional
event—a particular, historical, disruption of nature. It is not
an analogy or a parable of some universal transfiguration.
The world has fallen prey to death in all the gruesome reality of the Rwanda police killing twelve hundred in a church,
or of bodies buried in Bosnia or beneath a Mississippi dam.
Death for now remains outside *regnum Christi.*

On closer view, Paul does not alter historic normative
Judaism in the theology of death:

Deuteronomy 32:39: See now that I, even I, am he;
there is no god besides me.
I kill and I make alive.

1 Samuel 2:6*a:* The LORD kills and brings to life.

Psalm 104:29*b*-30*a:* When you take away their breath,
they die
and return to their dust.
When you send forth your spirit, they
are created.

Judaism, and especially apocalyptic Judaism, remains intact
in Paul's theology of death. As Rabbi Sherwin has written,

"The primary directive of Hebrew Scriptures is the challenge of sanctifying life, rather than escaping or being preoccupied with death. . . . The candid confrontation with death should serve as an entree to spiritual self-examination."[6] The intertestamental book, 2 Esdras, shows the florid and baroque imagery of this tradition, which also has bearing on Paul's formulation:

> "If I have found favour with you, my lord," I said, "make this also plain to me: at death, when each one of us gives back his soul, shall we be kept in peace until the time when you begin to create your new world, or does our torment begin at once?"
>
> "That too I will explain to you," he replied. "Do not, however, include yourself among those who have despised my law, nor count yourself with those who are to be tormented. You after all have a treasure of good works stored up with the Most High, though you will not be shown it until the last days. But now to speak of death: when the Most High has pronounced final sentence for a person to die, the spirit leaves the body to return to the One who first gave it, that it may render adoration to the glory of the Most High. As for those who have scornfully rejected the ways of the Most High, who have spurned his law, and who hate the godfearing, their spirits enter no settled abode, but from then on must wander in torment, endless grief, and sorrow. And this for seven reasons. First, they have held in contempt the law of the Most High. Secondly, they have lost their chance of making a full repentance and so gaining life. Thirdly, they can see the reward in store for those who have trusted the covenants of the Most High. Fourthly, they begin to think of the torment that awaits them at the end. Fifthly, they see that angels are guarding the abode of the other souls in undisturbed peace. Sixthly, they see that they are soon to enter into torment. The seventh cause for grief, the greatest cause of all, is this: at the sight of the Most High in his glory, they break down in shame, waste away in remorse, and shrivel with fear, remembering how they sinned against him in their lifetime and how they are soon to be brought before him for judgement on the last day.

"As for those who have kept to the ways of the Most High, this is what is appointed for them when their time comes to leave their mortal bodies. During their stay on the earth they served the Most High in spite of great hardship and constant danger, and kept to the last letter the law given them by the Lawgiver. Therefore the decision is this: they shall rejoice greatly to see the glory of God, who will receive them as his own, and they shall enter into rest through seven appointed stages. The first stage is their victory in the long struggle against their innate impulse to evil, so that it did not lead them astray from life into death. The second is to see the souls of the wicked wandering endlessly and the punishment awaiting them. The third is seeing the good report given of them by their Maker, that while they were alive they kept the law entrusted to them. The fourth is to understand the rest which they are now to share in the storehouses, guarded by angels in undisturbed peace, and the glory awaiting them in the next age. The fifth is the contrast between the corruptible world from which they have joyfully escaped and the future life that is to be their possession, between the cramped, arduous existence from which they have been set free and the spacious life which will soon be theirs to delight in for ever and ever. The sixth will be the revelation that they are to shine like stars, never to fade or die, with faces radiant as the sun. The seventh stage, the greatest of them all, will be the confident and joyful assurance which will be theirs, free from all fear and shame, as they press forward to see face to face the One whom they served in their lifetime, and from whom they are now to receive their reward in glory." (7:75-98 REB)

Beyond this mystically elaborate text, the biblical message finds disease, death, and sin as permanent stigmata in the creation. They are wounds that invoke effective remorse and desire for resolution. In the rupture where eternity cuts across or culminates this dispensation of space and time, illness will be banished and death overwhelmed. But for now, sin and death remain, though released from their terrible sting. Christ's reign and the enigmatic "first fruit" ultimately will conquer death. But at this time, eternal life and living life in love displace the resurrection of the dead.

The Scripture, like life itself, is real, brutally real. Theology B prompts scientific heroism and distracting hedonism, just as Theology A distorts authentic godliness and humanness. Dr. Kevorkian's obsessive experimenting intrigue, morbid fascination, and the seizing of the agenda from death, reflect Theology B. But Paul has opened a *via media* between Theologies A and B, between unreality and brutality. In rejecting ecstatic exaltation and earth-bound epicureanism, Paul invites us to responsible living and dying in gratitude and justice—the balance of *joie de vivre* and readiness, in due season, to relinquish life in the body to life in God.

Theology C: "Live and die generously."

Magnanimitas was the title of a book by Sir William Osler, who probably was the inspiration for the doctor at Johns Hopkins who treated Horace Giddens in Lillian Hellman's play. *Magnanimity* is the wonderful word used by President Abraham Lincoln at his second inaugural address, when he mingled justice and mercy so gently in the new disposition required to bind up the nation's wounds. *Megalopsuchia* in Aristotle becomes the medieval virtue of great soul, where one stares in the face of tragedy and death with a courage and trust that affirms goodness in life and its giver, and gratitude even when those mercies fail. We live in a twilight world, a dark world where the stars of eternity and God's renewed and perfected kingdom are still light years away. The world remains desolate and forsaken by God. In the metaphor of *Krebs*, cancer death still has us in its claws and pincers. AIDS is the enigmatic and paradigmatic death of the end of this millennium. It is an ignominious, disgraceful death—the cruciform death, like Grünewald's crucifix, the leprous lamb stained with the Kaposi's blemishes of Isaiah's vision in chapter 53. But those wounds make whole, those stripes heal.

The visual literature of our day, the film, best tells the tale of incarnate word, the truth of life. Director Jonathan Demme has given us a glimpse of sin, death, and eternity in his picture of Andy, portrayed by Tom Hanks in *Philadelphia*. The film depicts a sin-sick and death-bound world of personal wayward-ness and collective brutality. The film exemplifies the central legal text used to defend Andy, who has been fired from Philadelphia's preeminent law firm because he has AIDS.

Because of prejudice, the social death of AIDS victims occurs long before the physical death. The apex and epiphany of the story is shown in one of the loveliest scenes ever created in visual literature. Andy is beginning the moribund phase of his illness. In neurotropic burden and weakness, short of breath and wracked with pain, he is fading in and out of the beyond. His lawyer, Joe Miller, played by Denzel Washington, comes to his apartment to rehearse his final testimony for trial. Joe is obsessed with business; Andy is moving toward God.

"Do you pray?" Andy asks his lawyer.

"Yes, I pray."

"For what?"

"For my baby daughter to be healthy, for the Phillies to win." He betrays *deus ex machina*, God of the gaps.

The film then shifts into a surreal mood, reminiscent of Gabriel Fauré in the *Requiem* or *Cantique*, where earth's pain is lifted to heaven, or as was said of Fauré's music, heaven's pure breath is drawn to earth. On the stereo, Andy is playing the central scene from Giordano's opera *Andrea Chénier*. Maddalena has come home in revolutionary France to find her home desolate and her mother dead. Andy's plight and ours in this desolate and unjust world is depicted in parable. Maddalena wails in lament into the dark heav-ens. Then the music transforms into a blessed epiphany.

Death is actualized in the world out of the labyrinth of personal and social guilt. The child is shot at the Robert

Taylor Homes—the young mother dies of cancer—the heart of the just-retired steelworker fails.

Magnanimity is the mood and manner of synthesizing all these elements. It is looking death squarely in face, then moving through it in grace toward the saving power of God.

Theology C and Laurie hold this magnanimity—lusty for life, big-souled toward death. Her diary continues:

> Facing death is like facing marriage. You have to be willing to communicate with the doctor or whoever is there. Sometimes you don't have a big choice about who you talk to. But if you don't communicate you'll have a lot of trouble in dealing with life; you'll find yourself in a bind lots of times. If you don't ask questions to find out things, you'll always be wondering and not able to learn. Doctors and family have no right to keep anything from you. When you are sick or dying, tell people. Because you'll find out how many people there are who care, more than you can ever imagine, people you thought would never concern themselves. They often become your truest friends.
>
> Death is a joyous occasion—something beautiful. I am where we'll all be. If God made this world this beautiful, what must it be like to be there. We should all think about that before it happens. The biggest goal in my life right now is to get out of here. Jesus is like a goal to me, a leader, someone to look up to, someone I want to be like. I'm anxious to meet him.

The climax of Andy's trial turns on whether with his failing eyes he can really see the Kaposi's lesion on his head. Weak and stumbling, he is asked before the whole court to take off his shirt and bare his chest, showing the many deep blue Kaposi's stigmata.

> Now to him who is able to keep you from falling, and to make you stand without blemish in the presence of his glory with rejoicing, to the only God our Savior, through Jesus Christ our Lord, be glory, majesty, power, and authority, before all time and now and forever. Amen. (Jude 24-25)

Exploring Some Solutions

"Are we really caught between intubation and assisted suicide? Isn't there another way out?"

In chapter 1, we discussed a triad of societal forces (legal, technological, and economic) that can act for good or ill, but in the matter of dying have usually increased the burden of harm for many in our society. In presenting particulars of these forces, we introduced the dark and the light of each: that the law can protect individual rights as well as smother medical or personal initiative; that technology can empower care if used with knowledge and attention; that economics drives social and political organizations but is a force that in dying must be tackled at the level of individual choice of resources, as well as national provision for the vulnerable.

In this coda we present not only a bright call for the rarely heard concept of a cultural reformation that reorients our way of regarding each of these areas, but also four thoughtful perspectives on how this transformation of the national will might be *effected. Before attempting to answer the obvious question, "Is such a humanizing transformation possible?" or even examining the practical studies that follow in chapters 4, 5, and 6, we must deal with each of these sections in turn. In the first, we ask: What are the components of a "coherent ethic of life"? Must it necessarily be theologically grounded, or does this ethic as Ramsey, Bernardin, and Hesburgh express it, have universal appeal? That is, should (or might) Hesburgh's plea to "honor the weak and vulnerable" in our society become a national, multivocal cry?*

The second section, on rhetoric, asks this question from a different angle. Michael Hyde speaks of the "rhetoric of euthanasia," which refers not only to what is said (the creation of a speech or a policy, or an advertisement for a medical facility) but also to "moral ecology," the perceived cultural elements that drive the rhetoric. Is Hyde right about the power of rhetoric? More, is he right that rhetoric can create a shared national conscience if it is used as a means of dialogue? Is his idea of "normative discourse" one that can be universally applied in our diverse and increasingly uneducated society? What is the role of "acknowledgment" in the development—or the understanding—of rhetoric?

The third section tackles the law once again. Is it a fair analysis to say that law "approximates" covenant in our market-driven, rights-infused (disabled?) society? Is Goldblatt correct in seeing the movement of patient-physician relations from paternalism to patient-centered authority, to a new paternalism that is bound by economics and the law? Is the situation she describes one in which patients request more treatment than doctors (newly sensitized to costs and to the end-of-life issues) deem wise or efficacious? She speaks of the need to define more precisely physician and family rights, and community and constitutional rights. Who is to do this and how? Wiet offers a slightly more optimistic picture of a patient's power of choice. He also faces our earlier question (posed about rhetoric) of access of knowledge to the poor or the marginally literate. He speaks of the "congregations and other voluntary, private agencies" that might provide such education. How might such programs be implemented?

To even attempt such voluntary programs as Wiet suggests places us squarely back where we must confront the idea of "the common good" and the articulation of—and challenge to—social policy. Callahan's "naturalistic and rationalistic" position in the face of "increased longevity, burgeoning technology, and limited resources," offers two suggestions that he grounds in common sense and, again, the common good. First, we should limit life-prolonging medical interventions for the aged. Second, we should consider, as individuals and as families, what might be humane, responsible, and societally just processes of dying.

What do we think of Callahan's suggestions that in tackling these points, we should begin at the "desired end," peaceful death? What do we make of Callahan's criteria for a "peaceful death"? Is this concept one that is powerful enough, and universal enough, to gain the "national consensus" of which Hyde speaks? Within this understanding, are physicians adequately affirmed in their desire to provide case-by-case for a patient's peaceful dying?

Early in our project on "Dying Well," the Center for Ethics posed the crisis in dying well as a challenge to avoid either of two exaggerated distortions—the distortion of uncritically consuming whatever life- (or death-) prolonging technology was at hand, or conceding to Dr. Kevorkian for assisted or unaided suicide. In America and Western Europe, suicide, homicide, and concealed varieties of these two (accidents, alcoholism, cigarette smoking, obesity, etc.) now constitute a major portion of cumulative deaths, showing that a subtle transformation is already occurring in the way we choose to die.

We cry out for and demand more, yet ultimately need to undo that access and accept less. Mickey Mantle died the weekend we wrote this section. The social ethos heralded his heroism, much like his courageous baseball career, in fighting against liver disease inflicted by malignant overlay on years of alcohol abuse. The society, medical establishment, and finally even Lovers Lane United Methodist Church in Dallas, at his funeral extolled his will, "fighting to the end." The irony is that all three sectors—society, medicine, and religion—knew from the beginning that the fight was futile and unrealistic. But we must "go for it" as everyone expects, because everyone knows subconsciously that unacknowledged death must hold sway.

The solution and resolution of this quandary can come only through a cultural reformation that will transform all parts—social, scientific, and spiritual—into a new outlook of belief and value. Only such reform can save our civilization from complete degradation as we accede to the powers of this world. Our project found glimpses of such transformation as we observed grassroots activities that offered redeeming ways for us to go and so avoid this horror.

Society: "Honor the Vulnerable."

Many years ago I asked my mentor, Paul Ramsey, if he thought that the renewed antiabortion sentiment, reflected for example in the resurgent "right-to-life" movement, might have been an act of moral compensation in light of the senseless killing of children in the Vietnam war and on the streets of American cities. Did we now affirm life to appease prior atrocities against life? I was struck with what seemed to be the inconsistency of a certain moral suasion that stridently affirmed capital punishment and the further prosecution of the war, all the while denying poor women in our cities the right of abortion.

Subsequently, Joseph Cardinal Bernardin of Chicago has called for a coherent "ethic of life" that condemns poverty along with abortion, war along with civil violence. For several years, Theodore Hesburgh, as president of the University of Notre Dame, expounded the same "consistent ethic" to Notre Dame graduates who were to become physicians: "We expect you as alumni of this university," he would say, "to honor the weak and vulnerable, to decry abortion, to honor parents, families, and children, to love and serve the needy, to demand corporate integrity and honesty, to strive for peace, to sacrificially serve the poor of your nation and the world."

What signs do we see pointing to social renewal in this arena of growing old gracefully and dying well? Our definition of dying well—"free of pain, reconciled to one's fellows, at peace with God"—synthesizes social, medical, and theological *shalom*. Is this better way yet appearing? With the help of Michael Hyde, we examined the facets of a transformation already underway as society responded to the euthanasia phenomenon.[1]

Rhetoric: "Everyone needs to be acknowledged."

A nation, Hyde contends, articulates its conscience in what might be called the rhetoric of euthanasia. What does that mean? Everyone in our community has confronted a loved one crying for relief of pain and suffering. Even more fundamentally, everyone has to die. Everyone knows that today with the many ways to prolong life medically it can make the end of life even more dreaded than it used to be. When people today talk about euthanasia, they are in a sense talking about themselves. Seeking a good death, therefore, has a lot to do with community and communication—educating community, acknowledging community, being respectful of community. Rhetoric includes these elements. It seeks to develop what Robert Bellah and his colleagues call a "moral ecology." Today we live without a universally accepted science of theology of death and dying. We are bereft of any measure to calculate when, if ever, one's good death ought to be allowed to happen. Without that science or faith, we had better be prepared to turn to and cultivate a healthy communal rhetoric to deal with those issues.

Hyde asks: "What do we mean by the rhetoric of euthanasia?" A recent document from the Lutheran Church, Missouri Synod, claims that "God created human beings to live and not to die. Death in any form is inimical to what God had in mind for His creation. Death is the last great enemy to be overcome by the power of the Risen Lord (I Corinthians 15)." The report continues to speak of "death with dignity or merciful release" as nothing more than "engaging in unholy rhetoric."

We sometimes use the word *rhetoric* in a pejorative sense. When we want to cast doubt on someone's position, we talk about their rhetoric. In cartoons, we represent our hopes and fears, we deal with where we are and where we feel we ought to be. Why do we laugh? Rhetoric has to deal with emotions. Without the ability to move people (Aristotle) from one place to another, we will have difficulty in persuading them to appropriate what we call moral truth.

The five canons of rhetoric—invention, disposition, style, delivery, and memory—have been modified in present-day media, our poor substitute for classical rhetoric. When was the last time you heard Dr. Kevorkian construct a careful and beautiful argument?

Aristotle believed that humans would identify and select

truth and justice from their alternatives if all ideas were given an equal hearing. The prevalent rhetoric today will be established by those who offer closure and moral excellence, and those who are able to sell that idiom to the purveyors of information. If communicators cannot find an equal hearing for ideas because they are unwilling, or perhaps unable, to meet the standards for effective communication, they will be disabled, and society will be deprived of their contributions.

According to Bellah, to enter the dialogue is always to be committed to cultivating the moral ecology of your community. A major way of doing that is rhetoric.

Thomas Green, of the University of Chicago, wrote of conscience as craft. We typically understand conscience within the current body of notions of morality. Conscience can be expanded to notions of doing your job well; having a good conscience means that the craft you offer is of benefit to others. Rhetoric can be a conscientious craft.

Coming out of the Greek and Roman civilization, Aristotle, Plato, Socrates, Cicero, and others found that society was best motivated by discourse which acknowledged moral ambiguity, then moved to conviction by consensus. Sissela Bok, in her book on lying, makes much of how conscience needs publicity. Conscience becomes collectively engaging as it confronts evil and commends good.

Rhetoric at its best, Hyde has found, involves the acknowledging of others. Its intentionality is always directed toward the other. Its mere presence is self-indictment, because we do not now definitively know the truth. Rhetoric does that by helping to cultivate the moral ecology—by getting people involved.

Acknowledgment is important. What would our lives be like if nobody acknowledged our existence? We are not made to be ignored.

"In awe," says Abraham Joshua Heschel, "we experience the way of God having said, 'Let there be.' " You can't reduce that. It is in those epiphanous moments that we get a sense of what lies beyond and how we are to act. With awe, we begin to wonder. Heschel says, "Wonder is the state of being asked." In being asked, we are acknowledged.

Hyde argues that it is important for rhetoric to have a presence. Not to agree with what is being said, but to agree that it can be said and that it might educate us, is critical to normative discourse. If you don't have a rhetoric that's operative, one that will lend you a voice, you're silent—and in law, you lose.

Hyde illustrated the importance of rhetoric in the moral discourse by referring to the dissenting opinions on the Supreme Court in the Nancy Cruzan case: "If you read [the majority opinion], you will be hard-pressed to get any sense of who Nancy Cruzan was, but when you read dissenting opinions, because their ideology and sensitivity is different, they will talk out a different rhetoric for the public. I would want that rhetoric there, because without it you really wouldn't know much about Nancy Cruzan." He quoted Justice Brennan's opinion: "Medical technology has effectively created a twilight zone of suspended animation, where death commences while life in some form continues. Some patients, however, want no part of a life sustained only by medical technology. Instead, they prefer a plan of medical treatment that allows nature to take its course and permits them to die with dignity."[2]

Another judge wrote: "Nancy Cruzan dwelt in that twilight zone for six years. She is oblivious to her surroundings and will remain so . . . . The areas of her brain that once thought, felt experience, etc., are gone." What Brennan and the other dissenting judges did was tell "person stories." Their rhetoric established moral authority and humanity.

Hyde's research on the ethics of euthanasia, viewed through communal rhetoric, has established for us a sense of what society must do to move beyond the impasse—legal, economic, political—that we discussed in our initial description of the problem of dying well. A new language and grace, a new covenant, must be developed.

Law: "Law needs to serve the common good."

Law is the approximation of covenant in our modern, market-driven, rights-infused milieu. We find ourselves today in a world that is a plethora of conflicting and competing interests, where finding what John Dewey called a "common faith" becomes nearly impossible. Even settling on a workable consensus in innumerable public issues has become so difficult that politics has become a charade.

We invited two leading medico-legal scholars to open for us the changing horizon of law vis-à-vis death and dying, concentrating respectively on the body of case precedent and administrative policy. We asked Ann Dudley-Goldblatt and Mitchell Wiet to outline for us what new syntheses of human rights and community allowance are emerging in our time.[3] Goldblatt, an instructor in bioethics and medical jurisprudence at the University of Chicago, reviewed a series of some seventy landmark "care of the dying" cases, from Karen Quinlan to Baby K. She found there a movement from an age of paternalistic beneficence, when doctors did what they felt was in the best interest of the patient, through an age of increasing claim for private and patient-centered authority, especially focusing decision-making rights on a relative or proxy, until the present, a problematic time when physicians again have to "call the shots," their decisions now shaped by a body of economic and legal considerations.

The new situation that Goldblatt shared was one in which patients' prerogatives had been firmly established. The right of self-disposition of affairs concerning one's own body, for example, in abortion, and in "letting die" decisions, has gone so far in some cases that patients or their spokesperson-relatives request further treatment deemed by the doctor as futile. Animated now by cost concerns to curtail unnecessary testing or treatment and by conflicting legal imperatives, on the one hand not to "miss anything"

and on the other not to improperly "foreshorten" or prolong a patient's life, ethical bewilderment abounds. One can
be censured or sued on ecclesiastical, economic, or legal
grounds for "doing too much" or "doing too little," by "not
prolonging life" or for "prolonging dying." A kind of social
abdication full of passive-aggressive "we know best" kind of
judgments repositions authority in the physician, but that
authority is constructed and "boxed in" to the point where
it undercuts personal and mutual responsibility.

Goldblatt correctly challenges our society to work hard
and make clear its underlying ideological values about life
and death, about "right to life" and "right to die." Having
declared this matrix, we must then embody these values in
familial, organizational, and public institutions through further refinements in case-precedent law and public policy.
Where does personal authority end and public authority
begin? Where do physician and family rights butt up against
community and constitutional rights? All these fundamental
questions of jurisprudence—personal and society, church
and state—must be more precisely defined.

Mitchell Wiet succinctly reviews for us the body of
administrative law that now pertains in the realm of human
death and dying. This body of legislation and other public
policy has given rise to a mode of care practice that offers
greater respect for dying persons, larger participation in
vital decisions by patients and their proxies, and enhanced
sensitivity to public good when economic and technological
values threaten to override human values.

Wiet first reviewed Living Will and Patient Self-Determination legislation. For the last thirty years, we have wit-
nessed the gradual development of laws and policies that
encourage persons to render advance directives to indicate
their wishes in the terminal portion of their lives. We can
rule in or rule out organ transplantation, make disposition of
our bodies and organs, and declare ourselves on the use of

mechanical life-supports such as respirators or dialyzers. We can request or refuse cardiopulmonary resuscitation if our heart and lungs fail, as well as feeding and medication such as cardiac pressors if our blood pressure weakens. These judgments can be registered prior to critical circumstances by the early version of "living wills," many of which were couched in the language of one's faith commitment, such as the Roman Catholic "declaration of faith," or by the second phase of uniform standards on living wills embodied in natural-death acts passed by most state legislatures. Each state now has standard forms for a living will, assignment of proxy, or power of attorney at the end of life. Finally, in the new Patient Self-Determination Act (PSDA) attached to federal hospital accreditation acts, all hospitals must offer patients the opportunity to render decisions about their terminal care. Most hospitals now provide a packet of materials that include the standard legal forms of the given jurisdiction. Some hospitals offer this option in a rather perfunctory manner. Others find ways to offer consolation through nursing, social work, or pastoral services. As one would expect, the selection of this option and the utilization of these services varies greatly, depending on the socioeconomic and educational status of the patient community. Hospitals that serve more affluent and well-educated populations tend to participate to a greater degree in the informing and deciding processes than do those that serve indigent populations. The challenge to congregations and other voluntary, private agencies is to extend educational programs to the poor, so that they might enjoy the same range of freedoms and choices as those enjoyed by the more literate and involved, for whom the basic struggle for life is not so overwhelming.

Wiet then turned to the basic legal assurance of what might be called a right to care. This fairly radical stipulation of law, which would transform the health-care field if it were ever taken seriously, rules that there is a fundamental duty to provide care to persons who are sick or injured. This duty to care works in two ways with reference to care for the dying. On the conservative side, it grounds the obligations of nurses, doctors, and hospitals to seek to save and sustain life—not to withdraw therapies except for reason of patient choice, and to continue rudimentary life support such as feeding and breathing, even by mechanical means if natural physiological power is broken. In short, it obliges caregivers and institutions to faithfully enact their trust over life.

The more radical implication of this legal principle, embodied in the COBRA (Consolidated Omnibus Budget Reconciliation Act of 1985) laws of care provision, for example, finds that all persons have right to life-saving treatment, regardless of ethnicity, gender, age, national origin, sexual preference, or ability to pay. As health care moves further from being provision to being philanthropy to being privilege, this principle will be tested in the law, and the fundamental nature of the public trust vis-à-vis health care will be further defined. As we write this in the summer of 1995, even the mean-spirited withdrawal of social services from illegal immigrants in some states has exempted emergency and life-saving medical treatment. This may portend that it is a fundamental value of our society that no person will go without basic and necessary (not frivolous) health care.

These present features of legal change are part of an ethical renewal in the realm of social policy that impinge positively and creatively on the question of dying well in the late twentieth century. More choice enriches life and increases the need for interpersonal and practical responsibility. As coercion, necessity, and fatality diminish in the lives of persons, society's obligations mount. Today personal freedoms, especially those conveyed by affluence, education, and technology, are dramatically increasing, but regrettably only for a smaller and smaller portion of the global community. Informational and theological renaissance is expanding. The legal mechanism of our society protects and enhances human rights. It can offer recourse against parties that would harm or exploit. It cannot require duty or responsibility. This is the function of a more general spirit of justice and beneficence in the populace. To this broader aspect of social policy, we now turn.

Social Policy: "Might we not accept a peaceful death as the necessary concomitant to a social policy of justice and equality amid limited resources?"

Our project also finds significant reform occurring in the realm of social policy. We define social policy as that loose association of ideals, values, and programs which include visions and activities of communities, congregations, governmental bodies, and "for profit" health and welfare agencies. Systems like Medicare and Medicaid, Lutheran Family Services, Catholic Charities, and corporate computer tutorial efforts would be included in the cache of activities we call social policy.

In this realm we find the convergence of two ambitions: (1) to care for those who need help, given acutely limited resources in both the public and private sphere; and (2) a movement at the personal, familial, and parochial level toward the acceptance of a peaceful death. I will draw on the thoughtful study of philosopher Daniel Callahan, president of the Hastings Center, to elucidate both of these themes.

Callahan's book *Setting Limits* drew together threads of his thought developed during the twenty-five years since we first collaborated to create the Hastings Center in 1968.[4] The various sociological threads he has woven together include the acceptance of aging as a benign fact of nature, the reality of restricted economic resources, the irrational lure of ever more elaborate technology, and the courage and human moral excellence of accepting a peaceful death. Though no longer a strictly religious thinker, Callahan's thought resonates with the wisdom of the natural-law tradition of biomedical philosophy.

Numerous publications and conferences of the Hastings Center have focused on the proper and helpful place of the acceptance of aging in the larger moral scheme of things. "What Do We Owe the Elderly?" in March-April 1994 and "Caring for an Aging World: Allocating Scarce Resources" in September 1994 are examples. Callahan begins the study of *Setting Limits* by questioning whether he could accept his own recommendation of age as a criterion of medical appropriateness when he himself becomes old. Now reaching his mid-sixties, Callahan has stuck to his guns and has not backed down. Although we do not find as many sober writers in the mid-90s as in the 1980s (Governor Richard Lamm calling for the aged to move along and die; Leon Kass calling us, with Homer and the Greeks, to that wisdom where the leaves fall in season to allow new growth to proceed), Callahan has continued to elaborate this naturalistic and rationalistic position. His perspective is borne out in our wide-ranging empirical studies.

What are Callahan's recommendations to a society that seems so morally bewildered by the convergence of three forces—increased longevity, burgeoning technology, and limited resources? The heart of his proposal is two-pronged. As a society, we ought to limit life-prolonging medical interventions for the aged. As individuals and families, we should make decisions about humane, responsible, and societally just processes of dying.

Callahan begins by lining out human conditions and illnesses for which we should consider societal and health-care policies that do not offer life-prolonging treatments. Taking a clue from British and European social policies that discourage interventions like dialysis, radical cancer surgery, and long-term mechanical ventilator breathing in the extreme elderly, Callahan lists some classifications which we as a society might wish to consider to forgo costly and marginally beneficial life-support therapy. He suggests three: (1) physical

[handwritten margin note: Classic "cognitive function" i.e. an intellectual criteria / quality of Life for someone else]

and mental status, ranging from patients with brain death to physically vigorous, mentally alert patients; (2) levels of care, ranging from emergency interventions such as CPR to nursing care for comfort; and (3) quality of life, which he defines as "capacity to think, feel, and interact with others."[5]

Callahan contends that reason, common sense, and social awareness require that we approach human situations of aging, sickness, and dying in highly specific case-focused ways, looking at particular circumstances and making decisions to go on or stop in terms of basic quantitative and qualitative considerations. In the end we should ask, "Is it really worth it?" In our empirical research, which we will now review, we find that individuals and families, congregations and institutions (e.g., hospitals and nursing homes) are continually engaged in making these kinds of discernments. Because the developments we have reviewed in the social atmosphere are reflected in public policy and law, persons now have more latitude to make highly discriminatory judgments at this threshold of life.

Callahan corroborates his social policy recommendations with material from his traditional discipline, philosophy. Within this spirit, he calls on persons and families to consider the acceptance of a peaceful death as the necessary concomitant to a social policy of justice and equality amid limited resources. In a provocative thesis, he argues that "death should be seen as the necessary and inevitable end point of medical care."[6]

Initially, we acknowledge the moral strength of this contention that medical care is inextricably bound up with human life and death. Medicine should not confine its concern to life saving, life sustenance, and health. Dying well also is the business of the ethical practice of medicine. It is the role of medicine, Callahan argues, to seek a peaceful death. As patient, family, and physician begin a care program, they might start at death and work backward, he suggests. If the goal of medicine is to undergird a good life and secure a peaceful death, why not plan backward from that

[handwritten note at bottom: Only can determine what of a good life within context of individual's own life narrative"]

desired end? This will involve abandoning a harsh aspect of the Hippocratic tradition that physicians walk away from death, abandoning their patients to an inevitable fate and not trying futile gestures when the situation is hopeless. It will involve embracing the Judeo-Christian and religious perspective of accompanying persons toward death. "Death," writes Callahan, "is . . . that to which medical care should be oriented from the outset in the case of all serious, potentially life-threatening illnesses, or of a serious decline of mental and physical capacities as a result of age or disease."[7]

Callahan then offers a list of suggestive criteria of what would count for a peaceful death:

- I want to find some meaning in my death or, if not a full meaning, a way of reconciling myself to it. Some kind of sense must be made of my mortality.
- I hope to be treated with respect and sympathy, and to find in my dying a physical and spiritual dignity.
- I would like my death to matter to others, to be seen in some larger sense as an evil, a rupturing of human community, even if they understand that my particular death might be preferable to an excessive and prolonged suffering, and even if they understand death to be part of the biological nature of the human species.
- If I do not necessarily want to die in the public way that marked the era of a tame death, with strangers coming in off the streets, I do not want to be abandoned, psychologically ejected from the community, because of my impending death. I want people to be with me, at hand if not in the same room.
- I do not want to be an undue burden on others in my dying, though I accept the possibility that I may be some burden. I do not want the end of my life to be the financial or emotional ruination of another life.
- I want to live in a society that does not dread death—at

least an ordinary death from disease at a relatively advanced age—and that provides support in its rituals and public practices for comforting the dying and, after death, their friends and families.

- I want to be conscious very near the time of my death, and with my mental and emotional capacities intact. I would be pleased to die in my sleep, but I do not want a prolonged coma prior to my death.
- I hope that my death will be quick, not drawn out.
- I recoil at the prospect of a death marked by pain and suffering, though I would hope to bear it well if that is unavoidable.[8]

Personal wish has now converged with medical intention and social policy in a composite sense of what it means to die well. Let us move to a discussion of reform in the realm of health care and religious life, a reform that will make possible a new atmosphere of dying well.

Part Two

CASE STUDIES

Theoretical groundings in society, medicine, and theology invite empirical testing. If we are sufficiently troubled by the consequences of increased technological intervention or heightened physician conservatism, or the intrusions of the law into domains that once belonged to priest, minister, or rabbi, household, and doctor, then we long not only for discussions about change but also for concrete evidence that in the places where we go to die, change is indeed possible. The review of the philosophies and actions of Drs. Quill, Nuland, and Brody suggests that reflection is alive in the profession of medicine itself, a welcome return to the time when the arts of theology and medicine were blended in a concern for the health of the total person, particularly as death approached.

As some medical practitioners reveal their humanistic and theological bent, the corners of health-care delivery—until quite recently the sacred domain of the "certified"—have been entered by others in the healing professions: chaplains, ethicists, priests, ministers, rabbis, trained volunteers. The concepts of parish nurse, visiting nurse, and hospice, considered by some foreign or invasive a few years back, are now openly celebrated by laypeople and professionals alike, and in many places are added as a welcome bridge between what doctors and nurses can offer and the systems the patient or friends can activate to assist healing or to ease dying.

In the site-visit projects of the Center for Ethics, we did not seek to review every such cooperative venture or examine each movement in holistic medicine. Rather, we selected situations within three general areas where persons' dying is an abiding concern: efforts in the society, including "home" dying or home-dying substitutes; medical training and clinical settings; and faith communities. Hospice workers and physicians have been a central part of our grant activities from the beginning, forming a central dialogue group in our conference on "Dying Well." But rather than reviewing the (impressive) activities of hospice in the greater Chicago area, we chose to fund a study by one hospice physician, Dr. Kathy Neely, who has carried "change" one step further in working with attitudes toward death among first-year medical students.

Dr. Neely's activation of the future physicians' humanistic and reflective powers is echoed in the sensitive work of Dr. John Oldershaw with neurologically impaired patients and Dr. Eugene Siegel with the cancer patients, where at the extremes of patient distress the physician can turn the greater availability of technological resources to the service of a pastoral concern with the whole patient in

his or her existential struggle to die despite dehumanizing pain and (sometimes) mutilation. Finally,
where one might least expect time and inclination
for reflection, Dr. Cory Franklin offers "intensive
care" for the ICU (Intensive Care Unit).

The justification for the particular "home" projects we selected to study—one immigrant-Ameri-
can response to the dilemmas posed by dying in a
new place as well as radical concerns in the nursing
home—will be presented at the beginning of each
study. Running in tandem with each of these projects are others that reflect the dark underside of
the hope that one might die in comfort, within the
intimate household, at home. The findings on
death in prisons, death in displacement, death in
special-care facilities, and the death of young
blacks by violence put specific faces on what it
means to be deprived by others of the possibility
of "dying well" at home, with family, at a ripe and
appropriate moment in a life's trajectory.

Death by displacement, as with the Jews and
others of Eastern Europe or Armenia, can revisit
the survivor with alarming violence as he or she
attempts to make sober judgments about dying at
fifty years' (or a generation's) distance from a "first
death." Prison death highlights the existential
agony of death itself, one dimension of the dying
process of which we must be aware as we seek to
foster more humane and person-centered death.
Dying in a specialized-care facility can prolong the
agony of isolation unless physicians and staff work
vigorously to sustain and support their patients.
Finally, the early and violent deaths of young

blacks in America remind us that dying badly or dying well is not the unique provenance of the elderly or the terminally ill.[1] The concept of "dying well" in our society must be enlarged to embrace all—young and old, recent immigrant and established group, marginalized and power-centered. To achieve the possibility that each person might be free to choose how to "die well" includes, then, larger social concerns—education, housing, and equal access to health care, the law, and faith environments. How access to this freedom can be achieved and how differing sectors of this multivocal society might agree on communal "goods" may form the subject of another study.

CHAPTER FOUR

Societal Response

"I'd do anything to be able to go home again."

How can we create a "good place" in society for the dying patient, one that re-creates a sense of home in which s/he can find comfort?

While a general societal atmosphere is created by forces such as developed in chapter 1—Law, Technology, and Economics—ultimately the social settings where people come to end their lives are institutions such as nursing homes or home-care settings. In this chapter we will visit two such settings—nursing homes and home care within an ethnic community. What constitutes "dying well" for persons in these situations?

Dislocation and disorientation are two primary responses of the dying patient who must leave the place s/he calls home (or relinquish control over that home). This physical removal may have been preceded by the death of a spouse or partner and by loss of physical mobility and the means and ability to survive at a basic level. This state, which Ivan Illich has called the condition of post-technological humans generally, typifies dying persons more specifically.

We ask ourselves: "Is there any prospect of returning to earlier practices rather than sequestering

from daily-life activity?" Can we create "space" for
the elderly that somehow restores their sense of
home(land), place, and community—the "materials
of culture" that help us describe who we are? The
following reports, which explore two models for
dying well "at home" were presented at our 1995
conference in the context of four others: death in
prison, where persons "die before they die"; dis-
placements through genocide and/or mass movements of peoples, where the "topos" by which you
define your being and in which you take your comfort has been destroyed; deaths on the street; and
Holocaust survivors' approaches to dying a second
death. The sense of existential isolation that
attends dying in unfamiliar circumstances haunts all
attempts to create a sense of well-being or
"home" at the time of death.

Religion and Dying Well in the Nursing Home[1]

"If you ever put me in a nursing
home, I'll come back to haunt you
the rest of your life."

So cried Ellen, eighty-two, who had come to live with her
daughter and was dying from an inoperable brain tumor.
The daughter, exhausted from longtime care of her mother
and shaken with guilt and indecision, fell into a long spiral
of home confinement, punctuated by acute episodes that
sent her mother regularly to the hospital. She was unable to
care for both her mother and herself and eventually developed cancer of the stomach. Only now, some fifteen years
later, has she recovered her own health and purged her grief

at still "not doing enough" to ease her mother's last days.[2]

This story could be repeated thousands of times, even in 1995, when information about support systems such as hospice is in the public eye. Glenn Brichacek, Director of Pastoral Care for the Mather Foundation in Evanston, notes that while nursing home use is on the rise, the elderly continue to resist "placement," pulling against life and death in an institution as vigorously as did Dickens' Betty Higden in *Our Mutual Friend*. It may be that in some cases the near presence of neighbors, friends, and family, plus the availability of support from a faith community, hospice, home health care, visiting nurses, and the like make staying at home a real possibility. More frequently, the scene is not too different from the one described above, or even worse: the older person resists leaving familiar surroundings, wishing to preserve the comfort of dying at home, but the principal caregivers live some or many hours away, and the situation becomes increasingly perilous and unworkable.

What if a nursing home becomes the only workable alternative? How might a person then be able to "die well"? In his project for the Kellogg Foundation, Brichacek notes foundationally that "[t]he matter of dying in the nursing home is embedded in a more fundamental value question of whether someone can die well"—have an "appropriate death" or a "good death."[3] Except in traditions such as Hinduism, where this life is seen as "one stage in the soul's eternal progress,"[4] or Baha'i, where "we progress through various worlds of God,"[5] the suspicion that death is the end can poison the final years, the final days of life.

To expand beyond that basic fear demands attention to "seven key attributes," as Brichacek has summarized them from the literature:

1. personal control and responsibility (Quill, 1993)
2. comfort measures and pain control (Smith et al., 1992)
3. the role of significant others (K. L. Vaux, 1992)

4. a full and satisfying life (Carson, 1974)
5. a coming to terms with death (Aries, 1974)
6. quality in the time remaining (Hunt, 1992)
7. religion (Bresnahan, 1991).[6]

Although some have written that religion eases the dying process for older adults and lowers their anxiety about death,[7] little work has been done to identify the specific ways religion may affect the dying process.

How indeed might "religion" be measured in an older, or in any person? The terms *intrinsic* and *extrinsic* religion used in some studies have been supplemented by a third, *quest,* the "open-ended responsive dialogue with existential questions raised by the contradictions and tragedies of life."[8] Brichacek begins with an understanding of the interaction between lived (and now fading) life and associated religious beliefs and activities that includes all three concepts but goes beyond these.

Brichacek studied five white middle-class persons who reside permanently in a nursing home. Miss I, 84, is single, high-school educated, a member of a nearby Presbyterian church. Mr. E, also high-school educated, is 75 but had a stroke four years ago. His wife lives in a retirement home close by. He says he is not religious. Miss F, 82, is a retired social worker with declining cognitive abilities, like Miss I. She is a member of a local Baptist church. Mrs. M, who also has declining cognitive abilities, is divorced. She attends services at the local Congregational church when she can. Rev. H, 90, is a retired United Methodist minister whose wife died in the nursing home about a year ago. He is still a member of a local United Methodist church. His decline is more physical than cognitive in nature.[9]

The five persons interviewed were tested for "ways of being religious" (extrinsic, intrinsic, and quest-oriented); levels of death anxiety; health condition versus quality of life as measured against self-reported health; and overall characteristics (age, sex, marital status, education, socioeconomic status, religious preference, religious affiliation). Each was also invited to describe the meaning for them of the phrase "dying well" and tell what they thought might prevent a good death. Finally, they were asked questions that directly pertained to each of the questions listed above.

Brichacek's study produced three responses to the question "What does it mean for you to die well?": "an accompanied ending"; "an expedited ending"; "a prepared ending." "An accompanied ending" was the desire of Rev. H: "children and family around and slipping out—slipping out the easiest way possible." "Slipping out" spills over into the next response, "expedited ending," the wish of Mrs. M: "I'd go to bed and I wouldn't wake up. Either that or get hit by a truck. I want to go fast." "A prepared ending," Brichacek commented, "generally referred to the sense that something had to be done or accomplished prior to death":

> I would hope that I would be at peace and that I would die a peaceful death . . . to know that I would have forgiveness of any of my sins.

Miss I is burdened by "deep remorse" and "regret" for events in the distant past.

Brichacek was keenly aware not only that several of his subjects were somewhat impaired cognitively, but also that their responses were set in the context of an institutional facility. The question, "What concerns would prevent you from being able to die well?" drew three themes: concern with social isolation, as with Miss I, who has no living relatives; uncontrolled physical pain, which several mentioned; and loss of physical control, the abiding concern of Mr. E.:

> You lose control when you're in my position. It's been impossible to deal with . . . and this place is so unsatisfactory to me that I say to myself, "There is only one way to get out

of here." . . . I'm at the mercy of everyone. . . . You know, just anybody can walk in.

The "anybody" who might invade his personal space included the interviewer.

The five subjects differed widely in their understanding of "personal control and responsibility for aspects of the dying process." What does "control" actually mean? Is it nonspecific, or specific (perhaps the divine), as Mrs. M expressed: "Whenever He's ready to take me"? Or is this understood immediately as an internal matter, as with Mr. E, who prays: "Every night I go to bed and pray that I will die before . . . and not wake up"? Rev. H, however, thought of control as including advance directives that he be treated only for "minor difficulties," while being acutely aware that at age 90, it would be mostly external forces (the processes of nature), and not internal (the force of his will or his astute planning), that would determine his dying.

"Comfort measures" are a key component in the subjects' idea of dying well. Again, the responses divided into three: "extreme measures" (of controlling pain) such as an assisted death, or on the other side, the feeling that pain cannot be controlled at all. Miss I talked of assisted death, saying, "If I were in great pain, I might feel I would want that." Mrs. M, perhaps more independent and self-sufficient than the others, displayed "self-control": "I have a very high threshold of pain. . . . I can stand a lot of pain in my head." A third response was that of Rev. H, who, as Brichacek saw him, scored highest in all measures of religion. He believed that a faith in God could be relied upon to help manage the pain: "Here it seems to me, if you have a faith in God that you have to be thankful for that."

"Religious response" to the issue of pain and comfort lifted the discussion to a different level.

"Significant personal relationships" as an element of

"dying well" differed in some surprising ways. Miss I, who had shown concern for loneliness at the point of death, valued the importance of present loved ones when she died, while both Mr. E and Mrs. M described a need for some form of isolation. With Mr. E, the fear of burden (he himself had been "burdened" by life-and-death decisions during the deaths of his mother and an aunt) issued in a "protective isolation": "I just wouldn't want any relative or anyone close to me to bear up under it." Mrs. M expressed "insulated isolation": "I just stick to my own little self . . . and that's it."

"Life satisfaction" was a key factor that seemed to influence the process of dying well. Miss I and Mr. E had not experienced a long and satisfying life, Miss I's life falling short of her hopes, and both feeling "depleted by adversity." Adversity strengthened Mrs. M: "If you take those strengths and put them in the right places, they do you some good." This feeling of having been strong in tough times added to her feeling of self-sufficiency as she faced death. Miss F was satisfied that "I was myself," that she had lived her life by the values she had chosen.

All these people had accepted that they would die. But what type of death were they imagining? Miss F, happy with her life, felt that death would be "a wonderful conclusion," while for Mr. E, who had neither life satisfaction nor a high quality of life, death was seen as "the cessation of all worries." Rev. H articulated a religious response: "I believe my faith is sufficient to believe that God is the kind of God who has been good to me in this world . . . [and will be in] the world to come." Death for him is "part of the whole fabric of life"; "Work and pleasure and happiness and death are all part of life." A fifth response was that of Mrs. M—that death was an "adventure," which she termed (for herself or for the event) "curiosity."

What quality of life did each subject hope to maintain until death? Again, the responses related directly to current and past experience. Mr. E wished to be able to take control at the end, to

, Confession as outlined in
The Liturgy is important in a
"healing Service"

only individuals
r people

talk with "hemlock salesmen." Miss F wanted to be with family.
Miss I, "~~wracked by remorse and in need of absolution~~," wanted
to devote her remaining time to living a moral life. Rev. H real-
izes that he is losing his physical independence and counters this
by "reading some of the things I know something about, but
wanted to go back over them," thereby stimulating his mind.

How do the participants "use" religion? Brichacek sepa-
rated the "range of functions of religion" reported by his subjects into "belief, experience, relationships and practice to ethical living." Religious belief most often served as a "means to
bring meaning to experience." Belief in an afterlife helped
Rev. H to accept his wife's death and his own approaching
one: "I look forward to whatever the future has in the way of
death [about which I have no facts, but] in a matter of faith, I
do not shrink away from it." Religious experience provided
support for Miss F in helping her deal with a fear of death: "It
takes fear away and replaces it with love and the sense of God's
presence." The religious community and its activities had
enriched Miss I's life, otherwise devoid of human connection.
Religious practices included prayer, Bible reading, and attending services. For Miss I, Brichacek felt, prayer "confirmed an
internalized relationship with God." Mrs. M expressed the
ethical component active in religious belief and practice: "I
live according to the way I think God would want me to live,
and so far he's put me pretty much on track."

Intrinsic religion was found in four of the five persons,
most pronouncedly in Rev. H: "I think faith . . . gets stronger
if you practice it." Two of the five show strong evidence of
~~extrinsic religion~~, as Miss F's ~~feeling~~ that religion "replaces
[the fear of death]." Quest religion "struggling with com-
plexity, doubt, and ambiguity," is present in Miss I's doubts.
Brichacek notes that three of the five showed signs of each of
the three dimensions of "religiosity" simultaneously.

Nonetheless, Brichacek was able to draw some conclusions about patterns of interaction among life, religious

belief and practice, and dying. Those four who showed the greatest presence of "intrinsic" religion showed least death anxiety while quest religion seemed to stimulate death anxiety. In this study at least, this pattern also correlated with low quality of life and low satisfaction with life.

As Brichacek acknowledges, the small and homogeneous sampling somewhat limits ability to generalize about "religion" and "dying well." Nonetheless, the study opens a window into the experience of dying in a nursing home that could be explored further for the mutual good of both inhabitants and caregivers. For instance, the request for an accompanied, an expedited, or a prepared end of life are not demands beyond the will of administrators to grant, nor of recipients to request, once the options are known. Nonetheless, the participants in the study were worried that they would be isolated, tormented by uncontrollable pain, or deprived of control over their life and death. Surely these anxieties, now articulated, can be recognized and "managed." As Brichacek further notes, "the residents' own faith communities can be advocates and companions of the elderly in their attempts to redress these or other obstacles."

Of what benefit is such a study to nursing-home professionals? All five participants, even the one (Mr. E) who resented the invasion of questioning, welcomed the chance to reflect on their own death. The seven factors identified earlier as key in "dying well" resonated in some way with the experiences of the five as they thought about dying. Simply to be aware of the existence of each of these dimensions of dying—personal control and responsibility, comfort measure and pain control, and the others—adds to more sensitive approaches to older adults.

The seventh factor discussed in the story, the use of religion, proved to play a powerful role in helping the participants cope with the idea of dying. Belief, experience, relationships, practice, and ethical living—all influence the subjects as they approach not simply "death," but their own death. Any standard pattern of care, Brichacek emphasizes, should include as an essential component "support for the significance of these religious expressions within the nursing-home setting and a sensitive understanding of how they function for the residents." He notes the other helpful finding, that just "religion" is not the answer, that coping may be substantially helped by "intrinsic" religion (for its own sake) but complicated by "quest," if that leads not to faith but rather to a skepticism and cynicism that paralyzes coping.

In all, this study exposed a dialectic in "dying well" in a nursing-home setting. Dying can be both "active and participatory," yet passively receptive and acquiescent. Both "fulfillment" and a "potential for futility" were expressed during the interviews, and in many cases this reflected the life that has gone before. Yet perhaps this is too simple a summation: We still must consider how anyone can "die well" when s/he must die outside home, thus forfeiting the genuine control to think rationally about dying that might actually be enjoyed when death is no near prospect. Are there ways to re-create "home" for older adults who have left theirs? Brichacek's report suggests that frank and many-faceted discussions such as his among nursing-home personnel, and between caregivers and health-care personnel and residents, might stimulate honest declarations of anxieties and needs, and further the nursing homes' attempt to give not only "house" but also "home" to older adults.

Dying Within the Household

> "What would make me feel really good? To be able to leave this place and come home with you, Baby."

To many sons or daughters, this statement raises all the conflicts between affection and duty, distance and independence that so shape growing up American in this century.

Duty hints that as children have been nurtured and protected in the vulnerable years, so also should they take parents into their care when the forces of nature flip the parent/child equation. On an Indiana farm not too many hours from Chicago, a variation of this old pattern has been activated; the only son and his wife moved in with Grandma in the big house when her eyesight and strength began to fail. More commonly, noble attempts to honor ancient duties are sabotaged by extraordinary or even rather ordinary but conflicting duties: the competition for care with small children, or worse, young teens; the mother's job, which perhaps already has suffered by "time out" while rearing children; the young family's limited income or great expenses with college or mortgage costs; the anger of the other siblings, who may resent what they perceive as favoritism toward the chosen child.

A larger and more critical factor may be the size and isolation of the younger family, or the host child's single status. Another grandma slept in an outbuilding immediately behind her daughter's big house, where she could be heard easily and tended to by the daughter, daughters-in-law, and other female relatives who lived in town and often gathered to quilt or can. Not only did the family expect to keep her, they could easily do so; the "on-call" family staff numbered some six or eight, plus the children, who were not in a far-distant college or city law firm, but apprenticed to local farmers or, if women, married to neighbors' sons.

The family who tended this second grandma passed on that model of "dying well" to their children and grandchildren. Unfortunately, two of the family lived well into their nineties, with only a childless but career-successful daughter to care for them. The days of "cheap help" had already passed after the Second World War. The daughter found herself severely burdened by their care, with little but anger from her siblings, who blamed her for their parents' "early" demises (94 and 95, incontinent each of them for at least five years). She herself died in a nursing home distant from relatives and friends, begging God to "come take her."

So a complicated web of conditions and traditions may strangle any wish that, as a matter of course, a child might take in his or her parent. Not only is it exceedingly difficult to manage, even with the resources that are becoming available to us, but this is not the accepted Western pattern, either in the neighborhood or the community at large or even within the family itself. A child who wishes to try caring for a parent or parents may find forces on every side subverting the efforts.[10]

In the Korean American elderly experience, however, as an honorable death was often perceived as a reward for, if not evidence of, one's noble and virtuous life, the possibility that a child would not honor and care for elderly parents, or that the surrounding community would not support him or her in this effort is simply not conscionable. Confucius' assertion that "To live an upright life and to spread the great doctrines of humanity must win good reputation after death"[11] applies not only to the elderly but also to the young as they perform those duties that form part of their "reputation."

Peter T. Cha has conducted a study of the Korean elderly experience in which he examines these Confucian concepts of "honorable life" and "honorable death" to see how these concepts influence the ideas of the Korean immigrant elderly (and their children) toward life, aging, and death.[12] Glenn Brichacek, in the previous section, demonstrated the power of certain types of religious belief on the older adult's ideas about dying, and dying well; Confucianism exerts this same power or is even extended, as its ideas are not so much a matter of individual belief as an all-pervading system of belief and practice. Based on this study, Cha suggests ways the Korean American family, the church, and health-care providers can attune themselves to the particular needs of this population of elderly persons.

Cha's findings agree with Brichacek's, in that "dying well" is usually correlated with "living well" or "aging well." He reports that "how the elderly perceive their status in their own family and community plays a large role in their assessment of their current self-worth and past contributions."

> The more respect they receive from their children and younger cohorts in the community, the more likely they are to feel that they lived "honorable lives" before their family, community, and ancestors, and perhaps will be more at peace with their approaching deaths.

This contrasts with the economically driven West, where economic factors "clearly dominate over other social factors, where the worth of a person is often measured in terms of economic productivity." Where such is true, then the perceived "real" worth declines once the person's ability to "produce" disappears.

Aging in this system is interpreted as "loss" or "incapacity," whereas in traditional Asian society, Cha continues, aging is characterized more as "gaining," particularly in wisdom. Cha quotes from the *Analects* of Confucius:

> At fifteen I set my heart upon learning.
> At thirty I established myself (in accordance with ritual).
> At forty I no longer had perplexities.
> At fifty I knew the Mandate of Heaven.
> At sixty I was at ease with whatever I heard.
> At seventy I could follow my heart's desire without
> transgressing the boundaries of right.[13]

Cha comments: by this understanding of aging, "one only deepens as well as broadens personal knowledge about how to be human as one advances in age. . . . Advanced age is something to be announced proudly (in the life of a Korean, one's sixtieth birthday is one of the most celebrated occasions), not a regrettable fact of life."

"In the West," Cha continues, "one's filial duty to a parent is usually understood in terms of providing necessary assistance, particularly in the areas of finance and health care.[14] In Confucian Asia, filial piety required a much broader as well as deeper commitment." A team of Korean American researchers identified five main types of filial duty that Korean adult children are expected to observe. They report:

> Under such a system, filial piety, as traditionally expected, obliges a married son and his wife to serve the husband's parents unselfishly in a wide range of his parents' needs and wishes: (1) physical care; (2) social-psychological comfort; (3) respect for and consultation with parents concerning important family and personal matters; (4) honoring and glorifying parents through the son's outstanding achievements; and (5) faithful observance of important ceremonial occasions (e.g., ancestor worship, parents' wedding anniversary or birthdays).[15]

Rather than being seen as embarrassingly incapacitated, aging parents are to be "recognized as those who are worthy of their children's respect and honor."

For the immigrant Korean American elderly, however, this age-old tradition is in danger of collapse, and thus the "life satisfaction" that should accompany one's dying may be absent. Parents are no longer in control of the language or the social and financial base of power; familiar friends, neighbors, and relatives who once testified to the wisdom and goodness of the immigrant are not here to reinforce the pattern of honor; both the children may work—drastically altering the configuration of care within the joint home and putting greater demands on the elderly themselves. The daughter or daughter-in-law who once could be counted on to give her full attention to the needs of the parents may be on call at the hospital three nights and six days a week, or on an important case at work. Thus when the parents' health declines, hospital or nursing home may be the only option for the Korean American immigrant family, as it is for many other families who lack a large network of support.

If it is necessary in traditional (Confucian-influenced) Korean society to have this power, respect, and honor to move gracefully into old age and honorable dying, what might be done to compensate for the loss of "home" for the Korean American elderly? One Korean American Presbyterian church offers a weekly all-day program for the elderly. Between 55 and 77 older people enjoy a program of worship, singing, fellowship, and topical seminars, plus an ESL (English as a Second Language) class. The staff and other church members see this attempt to "alleviate loneliness and . . . despair" as a vital part of the church's ministry.

"Honor" here, as in the older tradition, motivates and sustains this ministry. The senior pastor has said:

> Elderly people in the congregation are an important segment. They are not a "group" to be ministered to, regarded benevolently, and all treated alike. They are individuals, standing in different spots on the road we all travel, and are persons with singular strengths and gifts.[16]

"Filial piety," highlighted in the Jewish and Christian context by attention to the commandment "honor your father and your mother," is thus restored as a recognized component in a "positive outlook on the aging process." Indeed, as another study of the Asian community has stated, "The desire to be honored may be the key determining factor of life satisfaction among the Asian American elderly."[17]

And life satisfaction, as Brichacek's study has shown, heavily impacts an individual's ability to "die well." What has gone before is not the entire secret to dying well in the Korean American experience, however. Again, Confucianism has left a powerful legacy. In Korean society, which has been heavily influenced by both Confucianism and Shamanism, death is not the end but a "rite of passage," a "leaving behind one's own descendants and joining his or her ancestors." As a result, not much has been written on dying and death in this tradition, yet certain assumptions about "dying well" operate strongly within the Korean American community. We must understand these assumptions, Cha insists, if we are to be in positions where we must care for the Korean (or more generally Asian) American elderly at the end of their lives.

The first characteristic of "dying well" (an "honorable death") is the ability to "die in one's own house, in the presence of family." To die away from home or "dying as a wanderer is something shameful that needs to be avoided at all costs." Thus the Western compromise of having Grandma live with first one child then another, in an endless series of visits, would be deeply unsettling. Associated with this belief is that "most of the Korean elderly feel that living in nursing homes is a great shame."[18] This is not "home." Yet dying in a hospital, one woman observed, would be considered "home" if all her family members were there. "Home" is not a place, but an embrace.

A second characteristic of dying well would be to avoid the long-term illness that places a heavy financial or emotional burden on the children. Cha reports the consensus of a group of elderly people that "a blessed death is a relatively painless death, coming at the end of a relatively long life." One woman observed that to her, "Death is like the act of going from one room in the house to another"—a "rite of passage," not a painful, halting bump toward an uncertain end.

The welfare of the total household remains a criterion in dying well for the Korean American elderly, as it was in the traditional society. The "good order" of the household, arranged by the elderly person as "leader," is essential. In the Christian community, this Confucian wisdom appears as a concern that they will have influenced their children and grandchildren for the good. At the point of *imjong* (the final moments before death), Rev. Kim noted that the dying person almost always instructs the children to "honor the surviving parent and to love and care for their siblings, particularly the younger ones."[19]

Based on his research, Cha makes three recommendations. First, he suggests further research in the area of the interrelation between religious/cultural beliefs and aging/ dying. Second, he encourages Korean American congregations and households to cooperate to provide "programs and caring activities" for older members, based on and guided by the principle of "honoring the elderly." Third, "filial piety" and "honoring one's parents" should be understood as powerful traditions, powerful commitments that shape the experience of dying well. Some parts of that tradition (filial piety) are unworkable in immigrant society, such as the primacy of the eldest son and his wife as primary or only caregivers. Recognizing this and other qualifications of the ancient Confucian elements should lead the Korean American church to work to reformulate "filial piety" in a Christian and immigrant context, "reconstructing its ethical framework so that it is sensitive to traditional Korean culture, to the current immigrant experience, and to biblical and theological guidelines."

For the Korean American elderly, dying well can happen only if the full family are present. Both one's faith tradition and one's cultural expectations strongly influence the way one is able to die. If it chances that death comes not at one's actual home but in a hospital setting, then health-care providers should remember that a "good death" cannot come unless the dying person is surrounded by family members—thus re-creating a sense of "home."

– CHAPTER FIVE –

Health Care Responses

"I'm back in the hospital again."

> Can there be such a thing as a "good death" in a clinical setting?
> Competitive medical school admissions can favor high scores and grades over interpersonal skills and intuitive abilities that cannot be measured in the practicing physician except in their absence. It is rare that the physician who attends us at our dying also delivered us, or cared for our children, or attended our parents at their end. We cannot and would not wish to return to a medical practice without antibiotics or technology, but we can attend to the training of those men and women in whose hands the care of patients lies.

Humanizing Medical Training

"Whatever happened to the family doctor and house calls?"

Within a few months of starting medical school, the first-year student has acquired a pivotal experience with death in the process of human cadaver dissection. The socialization inherent in this early encounter lays the foundation of a professional and personal stance regarding death. The Northwestern Memorial Hospice faculty provided an alternative experience for first-year students. Forty-four were enrolled in an afternoon of both home visits with hospice nurses and Palliative Care rounds at Northwestern Memorial Hospital with the Hospice medical director. Each student was asked to write a "journal entry" of the experience. Subsequently, in groups of ten, discussions were held with faculty facilitators. The contents of the "journal entry," discussion groups, and anonymous questionnaires provided the material for a qualitative study of the ideas and feelings of students at this point in their education.[1]

So writes Dr. Kathy Neely in summarizing the intent, methodology, and findings of her study, "Early Encounters with Death." Dr. Neely comments further: "Medical education of the last several decades has been noticeably silent regarding death education; however, within the silence are powerful imperatives regarding the norms and values vital to students in order to fulfill their mission as physicians." What those imperatives are becomes clear as she continues her analysis: to heal the sick, of course, but to include in that mandate realization that sometimes the sick no longer can respond to our healing arts and our medications, and they die. While it is more dramatic and "satisfying" to heal than to attend to the dying, this change of orientation, from fighting death to comforting the dying, must come to the physician-in-training if s/he is to be part of a "good death" rather than part of a dehumanized system that creates and perpetuates bad ones.

Neely's observations about the prevalent modes of training young doctors and the practical ways that training might be altered will resonate with the reports that follow from three physicians of long and distinguished practice who, despite a system of medical education designed (so it seems) to "distance them from their feelings" as they progress from initiate to clinician, have shaped their practices by the humanistic (and perhaps religious) principles that led them into this great profession in the first place. They are *feeling*, even while being efficient, progressive, and creative in their art. Dr. Neely, herself a physician of great respect and repute, has, with her colleagues at the Northwestern Memorial Hospice, set out to "clone" men and women such as these, who might retain their sensitivity, their awareness of the finitude and drama of human experience, and their idealism, even while staying at the cutting edge of medicine.

What is the current state of medical education, and how might some aspects of this be altered to achieve such an end?[2] The first two years of medical school are largely lecture and somewhat resemble undergraduate education except, as more than one Pritzker (University of Chicago) student has commented, "It's not as hard because it's all memorization, with little critical thinking required." The third- and fourth-year students' clinical experiences may come as a shock, despite prior experience in hospitals as volunteers.

For the residents, morning rounds test, with sudden severity, their tolerance not only for death but also for a narrowed idea of what "healing" might mean. Dr. Neely observes that these "trainees" (residents subjected to the grilling typical in morning rounds) "come to consider the obviously dying patient as uninteresting and unworthy of attention from medical professionals who have more pressing and satisfying things to do" (namely, to pull other patients away from the brink of death).

Hospice orientation and care are structured by quite another philosophy, as many of us will recognize, where "hospice/palliative care [is] part of the seamless cloak of excellent medical care, tailored to the needs and hopes of the patient and appropriate to the reality of the patient's position on the trajectory of life." This proved an excellent environment for the forty-four first-year students to experience death for the first time. There was no hope for "cure" in these patients, yet they could be seen to receive splendid care and affection. The students first accompanied a hospice nurse on home visits throughout Chicago. Second, in groups they spent another afternoon with the medical director of hospice as he worked in the acute-care areas of the hospital, especially with "patients who were in the process of considering a shift of their care from acute in orientation to palliative." The last part of the study involved the journal entries written by the students, several of which became topics for small-group discussion. Finally, the students filled out a questionnaire about their experiences.

A number of themes arose from the journals and the questionnaires. Students were free to express their "personal feelings," not in the context of regular medical education or in front of peers. Dr. Neely records the anguish in some of these responses:

> I felt very uncomfortable. I felt as if I was intruding on this poor woman's pain.

> I have a difficult time with death and dying, so being exposed to so many dying people in one day was rather overwhelming for me. . . . I could not look directly at them because their eyes scared me and made me really sad.

> The saddest part was when she asked me, "M___, can you give me a pill to put me to sleep?" Even though she knew that the answer was no, she was asking to die in peace, to get it over with. I was taken aback by this.

Dr. Neely comments that while students registered a "4" at "comfort when interacting with dying patients and their family members," most recorded comfort level as being much higher (16/17) when asked what they had felt in observing hospice care. Still, some continued to feel uneasy about being around dying patients.

> I don't think I could handle hospice every day.

> Going on Palliative Care rounds provided a sensation never experienced before in the hospital environment. I have worked in a hospital for the past six years, doing various jobs ranging from delivering flowers to performing CPR on a patient in the ER, and [in] all the years, I have never been so emotionally affected as when on rounds.

Dr. Neely comments that despite all kinds of preparation, little prepares students for the "range of emotions with which they would deal as a doctor"; as a corollary of this, the response to "palliative care" in operation "highlights our human and professional discomfort when there's nothing to do for a dying person except to be a quiet and caring person." That may be more difficult than being a busy one, with constant frantic activity masking and postponing our emotional responses.

A second range of student reactions involved "modeling," as these reports reveal:

> I think it is amazing how the nurses can deal with the fact that all their patients will die, no matter what they do.

> Dr. von Gunten offered his hand to the patient, which he eagerly grasped and held during the entire interview, showing the effectiveness of contact for the physician to evoke trust and offer support to the ailing patient.

> It seemed ironic, because to me, her headaches seemed insignificant in relation to everything else going on in her life. But it wasn't. Her comfort was an issue of immediate and significant importance, especially to the doctor. I was really impressed by his level of sensitivity. He asked questions in such an open and caring manner, displaying concern but never condescension. Most important, he truly listened to her.

[The nurse and doctor] collaborated and shared ideas and suggestions in order to allay their patient's pain, and it was evident that both greatly sympathized and empathized with this patient. Both took in each other's recommendations in order to reach the best solution for the patient.

Curiously, although the student praised this collaboration between doctor and nurse, students' reactions to the position of nurse and doctor in relation to a dying patient were overwhelmingly laudatory of nurses, but troubled by what they imagined must be a physician's reluctance to let a patient go.

"Letting go" formed a major topic of worry and realignment for students, as expressed in this response:

[I]t was suggested . . . that the doctors in the hospice must get used to giving up hope and be resigned to "letting" their patients die. And at first this seemed like something the doctors in the hospice would have to deal with. It was then put to us in a different light, that it was not hope that was given up at all, the hope was just refocused into comfort rather than cure. Again this view doesn't seem natural for a doctor to quit trying to cure his patient; however, in these cases I can see how making them comfortable is the most important thing.

Another student who found the hospice visit "very difficult" had felt herself emotionally both well-prepared and strong. Why was she so upset? Partly, she wrote, because in her experience "patients had always been in the hospital to be cured, but in this case, that just wasn't going to happen." She continues:

Another reason was probably the different role taken by the physician [from the one she had observed in her father and his colleagues]. After 26 years of learning that a doctor's "job" is to cure people, this came as a bit of a shock.

For many students, however, experiences with hospice comforted them and introduced them to the (perhaps somewhat novel) idea that dying people are still "people"—a third response, "just folks." The students "commented on the wide variety of human experience among the dying and the need for the health-care professional to accommodate patients wherever they were in the context of their dying." As Cha and Brichacek have observed (see chapter 4), a feeling of "home" is closely allied to attention given to the religious and cultural history in which one has lived, and to the presence of family and friends. One student wrote: "The patients are surrounded by family or friends, or living in the home in which they are the most comfortable, and at the same time receiving the proper care by a trained and experienced nurse." "Respect" for the patient as person (akin to the idea of "honor" discussed by Cha) is a lesson the students took from hospice.

"Intensity and intrusiveness" characterized the conversations the students heard. Students are frequent observers at the hospital beside or in a doctor's office, but here they were parties in discussions of ultimate significance: the dying of an actual person. The discomfort the students felt registered the intimacy and humanity of those moments. "I felt as if I were intruding on this poor woman's pain. . . . As time passed, however, I realized how invisible I was plastered up against the wall, camouflaged in my awkward new white coat. I felt like I was in a theater watching a movie." Another student expressed awe at the seriousness of the experience:

> I had never heard these types of questions (quality of life, feelings about death) asked before. Similar issues had been brought up in ethics cases, or related second-hand from family conferences; I had never been there for it. . . . It's amazing to be in a profession where involvement in these issues is not only allowed, but expected.

Only one of the students qualified his or her response to hospice. Most were enthused by what they had seen, as indicated by this comment: "As we drove back to my medical-school-three-block-world, I hoped that I'd do home visits as a doctor. Medicine in the hospital or doctor's office seems so limited compared to this."

Many students were profoundly influenced by their visits and consequent discussions and reflections. Dr. Neely identifies a fifth category of response as "Insight and Holy Ground," recognizing both the transcendent possibilities of the human mind and the reverential dimension of the doctor-nurse/patient relationship.

> Despite the fact that this woman was dying, there was no stress, no tension, no sense of an urgent need to do something. In this environment, death is not viewed as the failure of the health-care team. It is accepted by all agents as an inevitability, and handled on the patient's terms.

> Visiting a patient's home was helpful in really seeing them as a person with a family and life. Pictures on the wall, things that they had made . . . all told something about the patient and the world that they are connected to. . . . Now, no matter how sick they are, you are still a guest in their home. It is their territory and not someone else's, and I think that is important for them at the end of their lives.

A final question the students were asked concerned what they thought was the "best part of the experience." Dr. Neely has drawn three samples that express pleasure at being "exposed at such an early stage to such an emotionally significant part of patient care" and gratitude at being with the patients in their "living and dying." The final one of these identifies the following as the "best part":

> Spending time in a patient's home, being stuck in the middle of real issues like living-will decisions and helping a patient get to the bathroom.

Dr. Neely comments, "To think a competitive graduate student paying handsome tuition would find a special meaning in 'helping a patient to the bathroom'! It may merely reflect on how desperately a lecture-hall-bound student yearns for 'real life.'" The message of this intense and thoughtful study may be that we can see the kindness and compassion that medical students bring to their chosen profession and now can find ways to nurture this through the "long and grueling years of medical education." If we are serious about creating conditions where persons can "die well," then we must know that dying patients need physicians who know what that dying experience means and are willing to journey with their patients along that path.

Humanizing the ICU

"Do I have to die alone?"

The ICU is, by definition, a place of separation from familiar settings, from family and friends—a disorienting experience that deactivates normal self-protection. The patient feels a loss of power, not only over bodily functions but also over the clock and the calendar. Dr. Cory Franklin, head of the ICU at Chicago's famed Cook County Hospital, writes: "The modern American intensive care unit could benefit from some intensive care. As Sherwin Nuland has written, the ICU can be a cold, impersonal environment hostile to dying patient and family. This problem is critical but not irretrievable."

In his project for the Kellogg Foundation, "Complementing Life-support with Death-support: Six Ways to Improve the Intensive Care Unit," Dr. Franklin suggests that the ICU could become a more humane place for patients in the final stages of life if certain practices were

initiated. He recommends palliation; screening out inappropriate candidates for the ICU; discussion of termination of
life-support policies; employment of new technologies,
surgeries, and medicines for patient relief; humanizing pain
control; and personalizing the dying process.[3]
   Dr. Franklin begins his astute analysis of and prescription for
the ICU by quoting from Dr. Sherwin Nuland's *How We Die:*

> The beeping and squealing monitors, the hissings of respira-
> tors and pistoned mattresses, the flashing multicolored elec-
> tronic signals—the whole technological panoply is back-
> ground for the tactics by which we are deprived of the
> tranquility we have every right to hope for, and separated
> from those few who would not let us die alone.[4]

Echoing the pleas of Dr. Kathy Neely, he admonishes
physicians, nurses, other caregivers in the ICU, and hospital
administrators that "by neglecting the dying patient they
have abdicated one of the primary responsibilities of ICUs":
to create and maintain the ICU as a "more humane place
for patients in the final stages of life."
   This "mission" of the ICU has not one but two dimensions: to save life, yes, but also to ease pain. "Palliation,"
which heads his list of six urgent calls to caregivers, is inti-
mately related to Dr. Kathy Neely's observations about the
orientation of medical education. How does the physician
respond to patients s/he cannot cure?
   Dr. Franklin, while acknowledging and praising the ICU's
life-saving role, observes that "the best ICUs are those whose
staffs have developed the confidence to care for critically ill
patients and, at the same time, have avoided the defeatist
mentality which can permeate a unit after the inevitable fail-
ures." "Failure" is of course a term with meaning only in context of ardently desired, and confidently expected "success."
Mortality in "most" ICUs runs from 5 to 30 percent. Where

such a high percentage of one's patients are "destined" to die, then care for the dying must form part of the emotional and psychic equipment of the ICU staff, and palliation a "secondary mission when saving life is no longer realistic."[5]

How strange it is then to find that little attention is paid to palliation in journals and textbooks on critical care or in on-site training of residents and nurses. Dr. Franklin observes that "most of the attention devoted to patients dying in the hospital occurs outside the ICU." Because the need is so obvious and urgent and because so little is being done to introduce caregivers to this responsibility, he calls for a "concerted public effort" by "nurse managers, physician directors, journal directors, and conference directors" to highlight this need. As Dr. Neely emphasized when she studied medical education, to admit that failure can occur, and to broaden the physician's role to include comfort as well as cure, means radical change of orientation for those involved in critical care.[6]

Dr. Franklin's second prescription is to "prospectively identify specific groups of patients who may not be appropriate candidates for the ICU." To admit patients with DNR (Do Not Resuscitate) orders on their charts to a facility that uses mechanical ventilation or advanced cardiac life-support seems inappropriate and potentially cruel. The occasional DNR patient might need intensive nursing care, but most do not need the ICU; they are instead candidates for hospice. Why subject dying patients to the "rigors and ritual of the ICU" when they could die with supportive care and comfort?

How might such screening be done? Dr. Franklin suggests a binary model as follows, taking into account acute chance for recovery and long-term prognosis for patients with chronic diseases. Note that in each of the four possible scenarios, the physician and caregiving team are closely involved with patients in providing information and discussing options.

Acute Chance for Recovery

		Good (more than 25%)	Poor (less than 25%)
Long Term Prognosis	Good >6 mos	Encourage aggressive care Group 1	Provide information, patient option Group 2
	Poor <6 mos	Provide information, patient option Group 3	Discourage aggressive care Group 4

With patients who have a good chance to recover from acute conditions and a fair amount of time left, the ICU would be an appropriate use of resources and patient experience (Group 1). Those in Group 4 obviously are not candidates for the ICU. The problems in deciding whether to use the ICU arises with Groups 2 and 3. In both cases, the patient must decide whether to "undergo ICU care," after receiving full information on his or her options.

Most of the patients who would fit into Group 4 are known to caregivers ahead of time. Dr. Franklin lists the "vast majority of DNR patients" as "malignancy with metastasis, end-stage single organ failure" (among others, "liver cirrhosis, cardiomyopathy, chronic renal failure, chronic obstructive lung disease, or irreversible dysfunction of the central nervous system"), or advanced human immunodeficiency virus (HIV) infection. Who are and who are not appropriate candidates for the ICU? Doctors and researchers need to pay greater attention to this question as well as to provide advance directives that will "obviate ICU admission" and encourage hospice care for many terminally ill patients when this is deemed appropriate.

This does not mean that every DNR patient would be excluded from the ICU. Sometimes ICU care is a "reasonable undertaking." Dr. Franklin urges research into this area to produce actual data on "outcomes for certain complications" that normally require admission to the ICU (such as "cardiogenic pulmonary edema, identifiable treatable infections") and to "gauge the precision of prognostic markers such as patterns of metastasis in oncology patients, low CD 4 counts in AIDS patients, lung volume in pulmonary patients, or cardiac-ejection fractions in cardiomyopathy patients."[7] Only in this way can decisions be made that place the patient in the environment that best serves his or her needs.

The third and explosive prescription refers to the issue of termination of life-support in ICU patients. Whether, when, and how should life-support be stopped? First, we must realize that when used "appropriately," these systems ("mechanical ventilators or devices that support cardiac or renal function") can be great life-savers. Far from being "futile," or as some would contend, "technological last rites," these support devices can stabilize cardiac and respiratory function.

However, problems arise when the devices are used with patients who are not likely to regain consciousness, or are "suffering from an incurable condition." Dr. William Bean speaks of these situations:

> [T]he busy paraphernalia of scientific medicine keep[s] a vague shadow of life flickering when all hope is gone. This may lead to the most extravagant and ridiculous maneuvers aimed at keeping extant certain representative traces of life, while final and complete death is temporarily frustrated or thwarted.[8]

Such a situation would be cardiac arrest (loss of heartbeat and blood pressure), when the patient might be resuscitated but may have suffered brain damage due to deprivation of oxygen. The severity of the damage may not be determined for "days or weeks"; meanwhile, the patient is under ventilation but may have little likelihood of recovery of cognitive function.

What should ICU caregivers and patient families do now? The best situation would be to end life-support, thus perhaps allowing death to come naturally.[9] Those who argue that terminating life-support is no different from "not instituting" life-support are quite mistaken, however. Both staff and family are emotionally affected in this "choice and action" of "special significance"; this cannot be ignored. Staff must "devise and publish formal rules" that include "who is authorized to make such decisions and under what circumstances," and allow for dealing with special aspects of termination such as family guilt and "dyspnea"[10] after life-support is removed. "[P]rotocols on discontinuation of life-support should be part of every ICU manual, with updates and revisions as warranted by advances in the medical community." This is a serious action indeed, as Dr. Franklin cautions his fellow caregivers.[11]

These last two points, keeping up with advances in medicine and keeping the seriousness of life and death in focus, bear on a fourth point: that the ICU always must be ready to "employ new technologies, surgeries, and pharmacology for the benefit of patients." Responding to a famous case of physician-assisted suicide in which a lethal dose of sedative had been administered to a patient whose oral tumor was suffocating her, one doctor asked whether the physician involved in that case had thought of a tracheostomy, which would have bypassed the obstruction and eased the patient's breathing (and hence her suffering). The physician had not "offered" this option to the patient. In cases such as this, "relatively sophisticated medical procedures can be of immense assistance to terminally ill patients and should not be dismissed by caregivers out of hand."[12]

Some physicians and ethicists may hesitate to subject a dying patient to further invasive procedures. But Dr. Franklin contends that the patient's comfort should be foremost, and that surgery such as this (once major) has been improved to allow it to be effected "simply and inexpensively, often at the patient's bedside." To this he adds the "small, portable ventilator" which allows those with amyotrophic lateral sclerosis, such as physicist Stephen Hawking, to live outside the hospital. Computers can allow patients to "speak" with others. Patients may control their own pain medications. Improvements in anesthesia and surgical techniques have brought some major surgeries out of the operating room and to the doctor's office or the bedside. Antidepressive medications are more effective than before.

Dr. Franklin cautions against the other side of providing too much or unnecessary treatment to terminally ill persons. It is wrong to think that "nothing more medical" can or should be done when, if the caregivers keep the patient's comfort in mind, they could use a number of "state of the art drugs, devices, and procedures" to make life "more manageable and pleasurable."

Pain control also must be understood in a humanized context. In the past twenty-five years, there have been radical changes not only in available medications, but also in patient and caregiver attitudes toward medication. If a person is to be able to "die well," s/he often wants, and should have access to relief from pain. Pain clinics staffed by experts in this area are now available for both inpatient and outpatient relief.

What advances have been made in this area? If pain plus loss of control add to a patient's misery at the end of life, then the ability to control one's own pain relief ("patient-controlled analgesia") helps both problems; similarly, the patient might choose "sustained release patches," acupuncture, or delivery of pain medications through "nerve blocks and spinal delivery systems." The ICU would seem a perfect place to have such an array of pain-relief delivery available for the patient's comfort.[13] Unfortunately, this seems not always to be the case.

What are the anxieties that shroud use of medications for pain relief? An old one is fear of addiction, but a newer and more persistent one is that giving pain medication to critically ill patients might suppress respiratory function and cause death. This latter worry infuses the debate about "double effect" (death as a secondary result of medication) and "assisted suicide."

While critical-care personnel should be aware that these concerns exist, advances in pain control in most cases have gone around them. Dr. Franklin reports, for instance, that "most pain experts" would say that "with appropriate techniques, pain control can be achieved in 95% or more of terminally ill patients, without exposing patients to a serious risk of death from respiratory depression." Furthermore, in most of these cases, rather than becoming foggy, patients remain alert. Of course, in a few cases, patients may be susceptible to complication from medications; even in these, physicians, with the help of pain experts, may be able to get around the problems while still delivering relief.

All ICU personnel must themselves remain alert to new developments in pain control. Heavy monitoring and staffing capabilities make it possible to grasp new techniques and medications as they appear, and use these for the comfort of their patients.

"Dying is accompanied by fear." The kind of fear that has surfaced in research on dying is not the fear of death itself, but of being abandoned while you are dying.[14] Patients dying in the hospital often must suffer alone, either because physicians and nurses have moved on to more acute (and thus potentially more interesting) cases, or because a dimension of care lying beyond "cure" is not in their mental or emotional equipment. Nurses and other staff may perform their duties in a "perfunctory manner," imposing "every impersonality and indignity that the hospital can inflict" on these helpless sufferers. Yet this end-time is so critical for the dying person.

Why cannot the ICU doctors, nurses, and staff, so many and so omnipresent, "render abandonment of the dying a non-issue"? Dr. Franklin pleads with all of us:

The ICU should be able to offer a host of things to dying patients and their families, including expanded family visiting hours, grievance counseling, staff to facilitate the ubiquitous paperwork, a greater role for the clergy. Sometimes nothing more is needed than having staff take time to talk to patients and their loved ones.

Dr. Franklin cautions hospital administrators in particular: "Don't 'short-staff' the ICU. Some things can't be accounted for in time-motion analysis." Herein lies the burden and the blessing of his analysis. Some may think the ICU is about machines. "It isn't—it's about people." There is enormous physical contact between patients and staff in the critical context, and through this touch (plus listening, too often ignored as an art) the horror of abandonment can be removed. Trauma may be exciting to treat, but abandonment, and its accompanying night companion, fear, can be as difficult but as rewarding to treat as "trauma, sepsis, or the adult respiratory distress syndrome."

Where do these prescriptions leave the current ICU situation? Dr. Franklin here challenges Dr. Nuland's accusation that the ICU leaves "our survivors bereft of the unshattered final memories that rightly belong to those who sit nearby as our days draw to a close." If we were to bring back family doctors, we could recover that intimate connection between familiar face and sufferer. It is not, says Dr. Franklin, the ICU itself that creates the problems which Dr. Nuland highlights, but rather stress plus the dehumanizing conditions. Those who work in the ICU "may be searching for cure and certainty when none is available," and in the process may have left both "humility" and "humanity" at home. Yet Dr. Franklin asks that we remember that these are good people who, though they may not know their patients, can come to know them; who might currently slight the field of patient comfort and pleasure, but can be reoriented and redirected to find personal fulfillment in those parts of healing that are now overlooked.

The answer is not, as Nuland suggests, to return to a world that is gone and never will come back (and may not have been all that good to begin with), but to reteach humanity to those who work in the ICU and ask them to practice it the same way they practice their science, using "high touch" as well as "high tech" in the provision of death support as well as life-support.

"In the end, the intensive care unit is just that"—a place where we must care for those who trust us intensively. It is time, Dr. Franklin concludes, that "we make it live up to its name as it relates to dying patients."

Neurological Disease and Patient Advocacy

"I don't want to be at the mercy of machines."

Although by definition, terminal brain conditions shut off the pathways by which contact with other persons and one's environment are maintained, newer imaging techniques can provide physician and family with better material for making decisions about prognosis and treatment. Since the patient cannot participate in decision-making, however, physicians should encourage informed patient advocacy. The key element in patient treatment remains "close and concerned personal contact with the relatives and family of the patient." Such are the conclusions of this study by physician-lawyer Dr. John Oldershaw, whose study of three cases follows.

Dr. Oldershaw is uniquely placed to conduct a study called "Application of Ethics & Law to End of Life Neurological Conditions," since he is a lawyer and a physician with a longtime interest in ethical issues in patient treatment.[15] Dr. Oldershaw sets his parameters at the start: His patients, who have impaired consciousness or awareness and minimal contact with the outside world, are placed neither to interact with caregivers nor to take a major part in treatment decisions. On the other hand, the "advent of new imaging techniques," combined with conventional means of obtaining information about a condition, can allow "with a reasonable degree of certainty" what the prognosis will be, thus giving the physician and members of the patient's household a "more accurate basis for discussion and decision-making" than was heretofore possible.

Dr. Oldershaw highlights in his study the concept of "responsible physicians," which his case studies show to be doctors who take the time to review all possible physiological data on the patient and are attuned to the tragic fact not only that the patient is suffering such invasion and distress, but also that s/he cannot be fully aware of possible death—and thus reflect on it with the depth this calls forth. What also emerges in his cases is the attention given to all possible factors: prognosis, and how that impacts possible treatments; the multiplicity of cares available postoperatively (nursing home, hospice); concern for the effect of the condition on the family; consideration of possible deleterious effects of differing kinds of treatment; and throughout, concern that the patient "die well."

A belief that such nuanced considerations underlie all patient treatment shifts the ground of treatment philosophy. Dr. Oldershaw writes:

> The Hippocratic philosophy of medicine declares that nothing should be more important to a physician than the best interest of the patient who comes to him for care. This goal of medical care to overcome sickness or relieve suffering is sometimes obscured by the process known as "solving the riddle."[16] The Riddle is the disease process, and solving the riddle is understanding the disease process and eradicating it. This is the stuff that motivates physicians to improve their skills and find ever

improved diagnostic and therapeutic modalities. Unfortunately, this is often at odds with the welfare of the individual patient.

Dr. Oldershaw continues: "The art of medicine dictates that physicians have empathy with their patients and try to guide them in making decisions that will lead to relief of their suffering." That this is a complex process, particularly with patients such as his who frequently cannot participate in decisions involving their care, is illustrated by the three cases he has chosen to analyze.

The first case involves a forty-year-old woman with "severe diabetes mellitus with renal failure and blindness, for which she had been treated with a renal transplant and pancreatic transplant." She now had "severe cerebrovascular disease with frequent transient ischemic attacks," which had been treated by reperfusion of the left hemisphere with a vascular anastomosis. "Daily transient ischemic attacks" originating in the right hemisphere needed a right-sided bypass. After surgery she was "awake, alert, and oriented," although she had "multiple neurological deficits" and could not walk. A cerebral angiogram showed "occlusion of the right internal carotid artery and a left vascular bypass," which now required revascularization of the right hemisphere.

After the last surgery, the patient had multiple complications and was unresponsive. Surgery seemed to have corrected the presenting conditions, yet she did not improve. "Intensive supportive treatment" did not help, and with the agreement of the hospital Ethics Committee and her husband, treatment was gradually withdrawn. She was then transferred to a nursing home.

In this case, a severely impaired patient with "known preexistent illness" was treated unsuccessfully. Rather than continue treatment, imaging and blood-flow studies helped the physician and spouse determine that the situation could not be improved. "Sedation with morphine" was continued as

treatment was withdrawn. Although she was sent to a nursing home, Dr. Oldershaw believes that a hospice would have
been a "reasonable consideration."

In the second case, a forty-nine-year-old woman had a
"centrally located aneurysm of the basilar artery." An earlier
attempt to clip the aneurysm had not worked, and a "coil
embolization" was done. Before the operation the patient
was "alert and awake," but after the procedure, she suffered
a stroke and became brain dead. The family did not want
DNR status or organ donation. When she arrested, resuscitation was attempted but did not revive her.

This case shows the importance of close and constant
contact with the family. Given the futility of the woman's
situation, the family needed to understand that in this case,
"cure," or even "life" was no longer possible.

The third case involves a forty-nine-year-old woman
with "multiple metastatic brain tumors" that originated in a
prior breast cancer, for which she had undergone a mastec-
tomy. She was "alert and awake," with no "significant neurological deficits other than a dilated right pupil and weakness of the left upper extremity." An MRI (Magnetic
Resonance Imagery) study revealed the existence of multiple metastases, thus showing that "surgery was not an
option." Chemotherapy was not of value, but she could
have had whole brain radiation. After the risks of this treatment were explained to her, she refused further treatment.
In this case, the patient was judged competent to participate in decisions involving her own care and was transferred to hospice.

In this situation, sophisticated diagnostic techniques
revealed that no treatment would effect a cure, but rather
some treatments (such as additional radiation) might further
damage the brain and cause additional suffering. "In that
situation," Dr. Oldershaw judged, "she could not be with
her family in a meaningful way during her remaining time,

nor could she bring her life to a conclusion on her own terms." Here, as in other cases, Dr. Oldershaw thinks it critical that there be a "patient advocate such as a family member or a primary care provider" to work with patient and household to "interpret the options available."

What does "meaningful life" imply? The physician must not let his or her bias intrude, but rather must take steps to ensure that what is "meaningful" to the patient and family be fully understood. Dr. Oldershaw, reflecting with Mappes and Zembaty, writes:

> The physician must consider the values of all persons involved when advising a course of action. An ethical physician must obtain and reflect upon the concepts and desires of the patient and the patient's family. It is the duty of the physician to instruct them as completely as possible. . . . If [what is recommended] is contrary to their ideals and concepts, and they refuse to accept that recommendation," then the physician should gather other information that might help them understand the situation.[17]

This teaching dimension of the physician's role is linked with the "rule of law," which recognizes the enormous "trust and confidence and good faith" inherent in the doctor/patient relationship.[18]

Dr. Oldershaw acknowledges that there is "something unique about the human being separate from organic or somatic functioning," and therefore the physician must know "what is essential to humanity or personhood" in order to determine what death is. By physiological criteria, the cessation of neocortical functioning signals the end of life. However, since the human organism can continue to operate with machines, the physician must turn to the consideration of "humanity or personhood" and the larger meanings of "dying well," to refocus his or her care for the whole person. The physician who follows Oldershaw's cases and his practice will find a compelling model.

Global Management of the Cancer Patient to Relieve Anxiety and Suffering

---

"Please don't tell me I have cancer."

The fourth clinical project asks the same questions about patient care that were posed with medical education, the ICU, and highly specialized surgery and treatment. Dr. Franklin had questioned one suggestion made in the best-selling book, *How We Die*—that we need to return to the model of the family doctor in order to obtain personalized quality care that could help us to "die well." The models and the means are already there, Dr. Franklin had said; the personnel need only to be reoriented. The potential talent and concern are already in medical school, Dr. Neely has said; we need only provide them with the experiences and training that will enhance their caring qualities. High-tech diagnostic tools and sophisticated surgeries can assist the surgeon to make better decisions for the care and comfort of patients, Dr. Oldershaw has written, if combined with sensitivity to their emotional and spiritual needs.

Dr. Eugene Siegel examines the cases of four patients with cancer, three of which will be discussed here. Beginning with the premise that underlay the work of the other three physicians, he holds that fear and anxiety, which heighten suffering and may lead to a "bad death" (interpreted in part as a death from abandonment), can be allayed by the care that the patient receives from his or her physician. Dr. Siegel describes his model as "global management," which as he develops it is not so much "being managed" as being named, being informed, being treated, being comforted, and being accompanied.[19] As these cases unfold, we see how "dehumanizing" technologies and medicines, if used by person-oriented caregivers, can relieve pain, improve quality of remaining life, and enable a good death.

Dr. Siegel presents three cases in the context of a tightening economic pattern, in which pressure to reduce expenses (by insurance companies, by care institutions) and conflicts of interest among caregivers (to whom are the health-care providers ultimately responsible?) may divert attention from the individual who is ill, who may be dying, and who needs to be cared for and comforted. The economic factors may over-shadow the amazing scientific progress in cancer treatment during the past three or four decades and actually cause worse deaths (although the potential for more effective treatment is available) than if we had no treatment at all. Dr. Siegel writes: "The solutions to this progressive dichotomy between scien-tific advances and humane treatment of people with cancer are to personalize the dealings with such patients from the moment of suspicion of the disease, to converse about death from the beginning, especially after the diagnosis is confirmed, to unite the professionals dedicated to the treatment of the dis-ease, to decrease the power of payers and regulators to make individual decisions . . . and to accept the postpositivist concept that the knowledge acquired by religious revelation is as valid as the empirical and noumenal evaluations of the world."

This is a bold and multidimensional approach, but it surely is the ideal toward which the other clinicians are working. "Reorientation" of medical education or medical care means more need, not less, for up-to-date knowledge of surgical and diagnostic techniques and pharmacological resources—not to be used as ends, but as means to care more humanely for one's patients. What Dr. Siegel emphasizes, however, is that not only must physicians keep their diagnostic and therapeu-tic skills sharp, but they must allow themselves—and insist that their institutions and their society allow them—time to sit and talk with their patients. Cost/benefit analysis does not commonly honor this face of medicine, but what could be of greater worth than to share the thoughts and fears and beliefs that are appropriate to conversations about ultimate concerns—in these cases, a person's approaching death?

Dr. Siegel divides his case studies into the steps he takes with patients: suspicion of disease; confirmation of diagnosis; "staging," or determination of the extent of disease after diagnosis; and treatment. This "global management," as opposed to care that subjects a patient to "conflicts of interest" (among health-care providers), includes several key items: that one person follow the patient to the end of life; that in each step, the physician first keep the patient, and then the close members of the household, fully informed of all aspects of treatment; that all options for treatment be considered, balanced against possible increased misery; that the subject of religion be opened (respectfully), not shunned; that physical pain be relieved.

How global management might be applied is seen in three cases. John, fifty-six, had divorced his wife and left his family years ago to plunge himself into a "promiscuous" life. He had now returned to the area, where he was attempting to reconcile with his adult children. In the midst of this turbulent time, he came to Dr. Siegel with abdominal pains and a palpable tumor in the upper area of the abdomen just under the breastbone. Examination revealed a "solid, hard mass in the epigastrium," which could be suspected as carcinoma of the pancreas.

In such a case, unlike one in which cancer was suspected but by no means sure, Dr. Siegel mentioned cancer immediately, with the proviso that only a biopsy could seal the diagnosis. At John's next visit, one of his daughters accompanied him, and to her (as representative for the family) as well as to him, Dr. Siegel explained all the factors involved in the following steps: confirmation of the diagnosis; staging, or determining the extent of the disease; and decisions about treatment. Confirmation means obtaining cells from the tumor; staging is a series of tests to reveal how far the tumor had extended; treatment decisions involve consideration of all the issues that surround quality of life.

Dr. Siegel emphasizes that patients and their advocates may not be able to make informed decisions about how to proceed once diagnosis is confirmed, unless they understand with a fair amount of detail what kinds of tissues are involved in the cancer, from which organ the cells have come, and whether the tumor is in superficial or deep tissue. Both biopsy and tests for spread of the disease are intrusive.

For John, a CT (computerized tomogram) was used, which showed a deep solid mass in the upper abdomen, as well as a smaller mass that had been detected earlier by palpation. Dr. Siegel notes that the machine was able to penetrate more deeply into the body than could the examining hand, "using electronic methods unheard of just a few years ago." The surgeon performed a needle biopsy under CT guidance, which yielded cells that showed "immature but recognizable carcinoma of the pancreas."

Following his philosophy of global management, Dr. Siegel met with the family to fully explain the findings and their implications. No treatment could succeed; not only was the tumor large, but many studies have shown that "cancer of the pancreas does not respond to any method of treatment"—not to tumor excision, radical surgery, radiation therapy, or combinations of chemotherapy. "It is a consensus that the survival time with any treatment remains the same as with no treatment at all." These facts were reported to the family. Rather than dwell on this man's "past mistakes," as though this were his punishment, or undertake futile treatments, John and his family, under Dr. Siegel's guidance, chose to spend his remaining time preparing for death. He was admitted to hospice and received care by a loving and forgiving family. He died a "good death" at home within six weeks.

With Norman, forty-seven, the diagnosis of lung cancer required staging to determine the spread of the cancer and thus be able to decide on a method of treatment. This is expensive, Dr. Siegel notes, and is complicated by "numerous competing interests," which he identifies as patient, physician, hospital, insurance company, pharmaceutical company, and government. If each of these interests is divided into "duty to self" and "duty to others," the problems appear. For instance, the patient's self-interest is a long quality life, for which he may require care, even though he had made past mistakes (dissolute life with John, lifetime smoking with Norman). The patient also would expect to receive help from his insurer. "Duty to others" (to prevent disease; to pay premiums) is moot here, if s/he is already ill. By contrast, the self-interest of an insurer would be survival and economic profit, while the expected "other" interest would be to provide its customers with the financial support they need in crisis. Such conflicts appeared in Norman's case. He did stop smoking. Dr. Siegel also introduced a patient's related duty: to think about financial matters with his family.

For staging, Norman chose surgical intervention to remove the two known cancer masses. Radiation therapy and other treatments also were explained. The conversations postoperatively included the information that cancer cells might already have spread throughout the body through the blood vessels. Dr. Siegel introduced "death" in this conversation to allow Norman and his wife to think in advance of a possible recurrence of cancer.

With a third case, Greta, forty-eight, diagnosis was obvious and confirmation quick, not only of cancer of the breast but also of metastasis in bones. Even before the tests had shown metastasis, Dr. Siegel mentioned the word *cancer* and discussed possible shortening of life. The tests served as staging for the disease. Surgical removal of the breast confirmed that this was an advanced cancer. Treatment was presented as allowing not cure, but the postponement of death for perhaps a year or more. As with his other patients, Dr. Siegel made a personal commitment that he would stay with her until the end of her life.

The disease followed a different course in each patient, but in each it was important for Dr. Siegel and any other persons involved (surgeons, other oncologists) to know the patients' "moral and religious values" and how each thought of "quality of life." To be "spiritually close" with the patient is as important to the physician as it is to the patient; without this bond, the end will come as a "bad death." For instance, the strong religious values of John's family, plus the "magnificent institution of hospice," shielded him and his household from "despair and depression" and made possible a good death. With Norman, the return of disease threw his family into despair, but a second surgery to remove the tumors in the brain, plus radiation therapy, allowed him to work again and return to his family for additional support in the time remaining to him. With the third appearance of the disease and subsequent deterioration, he was started first on acute help, then on terminal care. He reunited with the organized church and kindled a different kind of hope. He, too, died a good death.

For Greta, this understanding of "religious and spiritual values" indicated that she be given a course of therapies that allowed her to return to her beloved teaching job right up to the end. "Mentally, she lived only for the school, and I knew . . . that depriving her of this would make her give up and die soon." Indeed, when she was forced to stop teaching, she felt "mental abandonment" and became unhappy and depressed. She called in her relatives and friends to say good-bye and shortly thereafter died at home.

What of additional therapies for either Norman or Greta? At Norman's third occurrence of disease, and almost immediately with Greta, to treat further would mean "excessive suffering" and possibly "more disability" with "very little relief." Instead, pain relief and palliation that increased comfort were chosen.

In this, Dr. Siegel again agrees with the beliefs and findings of our other clinicians, that undertreatment of pain is prevalent but "intolerable"; physicians need to be better informed about available pharmaceuticals in order to prescribe more precise dosage and monitor serum levels. The fear of overdose, addiction, or death is high among physicians, as Dr. Franklin has written, when in fact "less than 0.1% of patients develop addiction." *Addiction* is an emotion-laden word for physicians; medical training should include "better training in pain management," ignoring worries about addiction in a suffering patient who is near death. Dr. Siegel adds, "Poor sensitivity of physicians and nurses to human suffering causes inadequate recognition of pain"; his prescription for "cutting" this would seem to be that of Drs. Neely, Franklin, and Oldershaw: "Need for better humanistic training in medical and nursing schools."

What does his study reveal to be components in cancer patients' "dying well"?: support; virtuous love (rather than abandonment); moral compassion (rather than denial of service); scientific purity (rather than "economic considerations"); global management (rather than conflict of interests); societal approval (rather than rejection); legal assent (rather than exaggerated claim); insurance coverage (rather than refusal of services). In all this, the physician should be the "patient's best advocate" and companion in this last journey.

– CHAPTER SIX –

Religious Responses

*"I miss the music, the quiet, and my friends.
No one comes to see me anymore."*

How can faith communities best respond to the needs of dying patients?

A year ago, we sent out 250 questionnaires to Chicago and suburban congregations from a plurality of faiths, in which we attempted to discover what programs existed to address the needs of dying persons and their families. From among the 28 questionnaires returned, seven came from the suburbs and 21 from the city; half were from all-white or mostly white congregations, one-quarter from African American congregations. One Asian American and one Hispanic American church responded. The other five responses came from congregations of mixed ethnic composition. In addition, we conducted sixteen interviews within city and suburban religious groups that had well-developed responses to dying and death with thoughtful understandings of what it means to "die well."[1]

Not surprisingly, the programs reflected not only the belief system of the particular worshiping body but also the individual needs of the congregation served. Religious bodies reacted in each of the following areas with energy that ranged from prayers and phone calls to organized committees for care of the dying to parish nurse/hospice/hospital connections.

A constant element in the questionnaires and interviews was the perception that one person's dying and death affected the entire body of faith, just as the death itself has both spiritual and practical dimensions that cry equally to be addressed.

Rabbi Arnold Jacob Wolf voices the anguish and concern that motivate persons from all faiths to attend to their own dying and the dying of persons they love: "Death tests what we have believed about God and about life. It stretches our convictions and our trust; it finds out what we really are like."[2]

With these insightful comments, we examine a number of ways in which congregations and their priests, rabbis, or pastors have faced the wrenching issues of interpersonal deprivation, loss of worship, and lack of knowledge or inability to perform ordinary survival tasks.

The Healing Power of Touch

Each of the religious bodies contacted was acutely aware that hospitalized or home-locked persons are distressed by the absence of contact with other people. The dying are often out of the loop, particularly if they have suffered a lengthy disease or are among the elderly. No one says their name; no one cherishes their presence. Often, all their friends are dead. What they experience is early death by isolation: no more kitchen chats; no more sharing of dreams (the time of dreaming, of hope, is gone); no more cards and laughs at midnight; no more trips to visit family or even to the grocery store.

At the most basic level, then, what a worshiping community can provide is continued friendship—"being there," even if the patient's power to interact is severely restricted.

What is needed is a community to be present with us; persons who are grieving and/or dying need loved ones and friends who know that what they are suffering does not have anything to do with the depth of their faith or the way they have lived. They need fellow pilgrims on life's journey who have the courage to encourage them in the spiritual and moral wrestling that they are doing and to support them in their decisions, even if they would not be our decisions.[3]

Visitation

"Visitation" is among the oldest of established congregational responses to human need at the edge of life. To address this need, one urban church wrote that they "have a committee who are responsible to support any member of the congregation with prayer, phone calls, and help." The Stephen Ministry, a vital lay ministry within the Presbyterian and other Protestant and Catholic churches, takes the commitment of friendship and presence seriously: laypeople, who accept a two-year commitment, are intensely trained to be good listeners, to attend to basic needs, and to refer urgent cases to the appropriate source.

A group of 25 to 35 lay members meets bimonthly at Reba Church for training sessions in listening and other skills. Needs usually are channeled first to the parish nurse, who visits the sick, then assigns a minister of care. Saint Mark's Episcopal Church of Evanston has listening groups. Further, its retirement-home visiting groups are composed not only of singles but also of couples, older seniors, mother/daughter teams, and adult/child teams to ensure that the whole community is involved in the life and dying of its members—an important intergenerational approach. Saints Peter and Paul Greek Orthodox Church in Chicago has a similar philosophy of offering intergenerational contact.

Lincoln Park Presbyterian in Chicago has church teams that visit sick people. The pastor sits with the dying, supported by the parish associate, who leads an active lay ministry trained in listening and other sensitivity skills. These insights were offered: "Teams of people are believed to be good not only to help the pastor, but to get the congregation involved as well." "If they deliver meals, [the visitors] know it's more comforting if they eat with the person than just drop off the food and go." Reba Church, formerly an intentional community, has about twenty-five groups of twelve who visit the sick and dying. At Beth Emet the Free Congregation in Evanston, the *ozerim* ("helpers") provide outreach to the sick and keep the rabbi in touch with congregational concerns.[4]

Saints Peter and Paul Greek Orthodox Church in Chicago has a Philanthropy ("friend of the poor") group of women who make sick calls. The pastor and his wife emphasized that each person in the parish is a *parikos*, a Christian, and thus a member of a colony of heaven on earth. This feeling motivates congregational participation in the cycles of life of all members. The pastor of North Shore Assembly of God echoes this participatory mandate:

> Most important is the relationship that the people have with one another in the sense of caring. The empathy, the compassion they have for one another for reaching out . . . how wonderful it is to have the family that supports you and that's with you, and you feel like they're there for you. People are saying, "We're praying for you." They're calling, making visits. . . . I think people are just looking for someone with a caring heart to be there.[5]

The parish nurse at Reba Church, whose salary is provided by St. Francis Hospital and who has an office at the church, started a program called Senior Connections, a "ministry for homebound elderly people, and that might be just chats, trips to the grocery store."[6]

In some congregations within Reform Judaism, concern for the privacy of the individual may balance a wish to relieve suffering and provide comfort as the congregation responds to the sick and dying. At KAM Isaiah Israel Congregation of Chicago, for instance, although there is a committee of care composed of eight or nine persons who visit the sick and dying, visits by rabbi or committee would not take place unless the dying person or family gave permission. In earlier times in this tradition as in others, dying and death were more public affairs, and the response of the community was immediate, public, and all-embracing. This is no longer true in our "privatized" society, and the congregation members respect one another's desire to face their suffering and illness privately, if they so wish.[7]

These strict sensitivities for the feelings of the dying and bereaved resemble those expressed by a member of one Lutheran congregation, who considered calls, cards, and visits by persons she did not know well in health to intrude into her privacy, to be ways for those individuals to assuage their own guilt. Clearly, part of joining a ministry of care would be to pick up signals from the people visited and allow them their space, if this is what they require in their dying.

The priest at Saint Nicholas has worked actively to counter privatization, which could be seen as a self-imposed sequestering. He encourages parishioners to identify their needs, even to reveal their wishes at Mass, when they are able to attend.

Practical Needs

Beyond friendship, beyond worship, past the time for education, are the purely physical needs for a person who has lost the ability to perform daily chores. Who will cook meals, watch the children, clean the house? If family is there, how do the members keep from wearing down? (As Professor Vogel has reminded us, families often begin to grieve even before death, and the concrete presence of the faith community can help ease this time.) Would the person who is dying find a good massage relaxing? The Covenantal Medical Center Hospice Care Program in Champaign/Urbana, Illinois, has begun a touch-therapy program.[8] Awareness of the urgency of such simple items, as well as the need for pain relief, is among the many gifts of the hospice movement. Most congregations contacted refer their members to hospice; some have cultivated a relationship with one hospice in particular. Others may do so, but also maintain a system of practical care within their own congregation.

At North Shore Assembly of God in Skokie, for instance, the church connects families with agencies that will help them with their physical needs, but parishioners may go into the homes to help with light housekeeping. As more people choose to die at home, the church has added a ministry to mobilize members of the congregation for practical tasks.

At Lincoln Park Presbyterian, the caregiving team responded not only with friendship but also with physical help for "John." He wanted to die at home and was able to remain there until twenty-four hours before he died. This required a cadre of helpers: nurses two or three times a week; other household help; and most important, the weekly visits of the pastor and members of the caregiving team. This group, comprised of the parish associate and three self-identified church members, met for support and spaced their visits, passing on to one another what they thought John needed. Some of the practical needs were help going to the doctor or to the hospital, and just getting up the three flights of stairs to his apartment!

Reba Church mobilizes its Pastoral Care Units to tend to the needs of the dying. Usually, the most appropriate person will self-identify to help in an individual case, as a nurse-mid-wife might bring comfort to a family whose newborn had died, or someone with medical training might tend to the needs of a person dying at home. With an elderly man who wished to die at home, the Pastoral Care group arranged for twenty-four hour care, with people taking turns.

First Presbyterian Church of Evanston has three levels of involvement with (among other tasks) ministry to the dying: the "1-2-1" visitors who work under the deacons; the deacons themselves; the Stephen ministers. The difference among the groups is partly the amount and kind of training each under-goes, and partly the level at which a given person will feel comfortable. The twenty-one "1-2-1" visitors meet three times a year for a workshop, to train but also to give one another support. They visit the sick and elderly about once a month to "maintain contact with the church." All thirty-six deacons, who are officers of the church, visit the elderly, which at First Presbyterian is a significant number—about two hundred people are eighty or over. In addition, the Minister of Pastoral Care, whose background includes Clinical Pastoral Education (CPE), has active links with the Mather Homes chaplains and the chaplains at a number of hospitals.

The largest and most active group at First Presbyterian that may become involved with both visitation and practical needs, is the Stephen Ministry. Currently the Ministry has 45 active lay members who might see people in all kinds of crisis situations. Their 50-week training includes work with death and dying, grief and bereavement, and issues of aging. Nine Stephen leaders train the others, not only during the initial six-month period, but also in the continuing education (outside speakers, supervision) program. Although the pastors may attend the occasional leadership session, this is a lay-run and lay-done ministry.[9]

The most enthusiastic response to the larger area of "education and practical needs" came from congregations that have some connection with Visiting Nurse programs.[10] Saint Nicholas in Evanston, Saint Vincent's in Chicago, Saints Peter and Paul Greek Orthodox in Chicago, and Reba Church, among others, have parish nurses, whose roles range from providing pamphlets on a variety of services, to holding educational programs on specific topics, to visiting the dying.

At Saint Nicholas, as mentioned above, the parish nurse is often the first point of contact. She has her hands on all the resources that might be helpful to an individual and household and is able to judge the level of contact needed. Does the person need transportation, hospice, or home care? She might mobilize the parish to provide meals, as in the case of a young mother dying of cancer who had two children at home. On the other side of her involvement, she might visit a dying person with both the communion elements and her blood-pressure equipment in hand. She has extensive contact with physicians in the area, who are usually responsive to her assessments.[11]

Surveys

Among the congregations that responded to our survey of Chicago area religious bodies, most did have a plan or a group to address the need to provide companionship and help for the dying. These ranged from a "sacramental ministry" (discussed below) to visits, flowers, and cards. Of 28 responses, 12 identified no formal committee, program, or "relational" connection within the congregation, although of these, one commented that "there are cultural customs that help," and another wrote that all members of the congregation help in informal ways when there is need. Rabbi Peter Knobel has observed that Reform Judaism tends to involve the entire congregation in matters of concern, rather than delegating everything to the pastor (or priest or rabbi); a number of our respondents indicated that this, too, was their pattern of congregational care.[12] Pastoral care given by a "board of deacons" (or "ministry of care") can bridge the religious leader and the congregation, not only in offering concrete help with visitation and practical tasks, but also in recognizing that "all in the congregation share in this responsibility."

The Quiet and the Community of Sacred Space

Many congregations directly address the loss of *Gemeinde*[13] and communion (in the general sense)—the richness of shared religious life, the sights and sounds and smells associated with liturgy and ritual. This sense of loss may be as acute in those who have rarely attended services as in the faithful worshipers. Not only do the dying miss traditional religious services, but they miss "service substitutes": quiet walks in the country or in their own garden; ritual gatherings of friends and family; even a trip to the ballpark—connections with nature and with the larger human community.

Faith traditions and individual congregations within these traditions differ in the ways they carry "the sacred" to the dying. First Presbyterian of Evanston takes prayer and presence but not communion, unless asked, although regular communion is something the minister of pastoral care would like to initiate.[14] Beth Emet the Free Congregation brings prayer and blessing; as in KAM Isaiah Israel Congregation, the presence of the rabbi during the dying process is important, with prayer, blessing, and the holding of hands. "Like one whom his mother comforts will I comfort you, says God, and you will be comforted within Jerusalem," for, as the pastor of Lincoln Park Presbyterian has noted, the dying are impoverished by the distant and "gloved" touch, and nourished and spiritually healed by the warmth of hands and by prayers.

The literature distributed by KAM Isaiah Israel notes further that "a Jew is expected to die, as he has lived, with the name of God on his lips."[15] For Judaism, Rabbi Sherwin has written:

The problem of dying well is not how to die in a state of grace, but how to die gracefully. The challenge is not how to escape death, but how to sanctify life. The purpose of life is how to live a life of purpose that would make one's death a catastrophe.[16]

Rabbi Sherwin continues, "The face to face confrontation with death can compel us to set our priorities straight, to determine what and whom we value."

Jewish rituals related to dying, death, and mourning affirm "respect for the dead, simplicity and equality, communal responsibility, and the affirmation of life," what Sherwin calls "responses to the mystery of existence, to the surprise of being alive, to the confrontation of the reality of our own mortality."

At the approach of death, one prays for divine forgiveness of sins, acknowledges the sovereignty of God and the truth of Torah, and prays a prayer that acknowledges trust in God and asks for mercy: "Fervently do I pray and sincerely do I trust that Thou wilt show me the path of life so that, cleansed through Thee, my soul may enter life everlasting." (If the person is unable to pray aloud, the rabbi or family member may say the prayer.)[17] Dying in the embrace of the community and the faith, believing in God's mercy, is critical to "dying well."

The rectors at Saint Mark's Episcopal meet with the dying as many times as they feel people need it and direct them to hospice when death is impending. "If you're going to care for the living, you have to care for the dying."[18] The same combination of providing spiritual and practical help was expressed by the rabbi at Beth Emet the Free, who with his colleagues visits the sick at home or in the hospital and puts members in touch with hospice when this seems appropriate. The pastor at North Shore Assembly of God leans on the relationship his church has built up with a local hospital chaplaincy program, but he too provides both education and spiritual comfort, working through denial with patient and family.

Lincoln Park Presbyterian has taken another approach to providing worship for the dying. Recently the church has decided to install a three-stage lift on the back of the church to allow members who are weak and/or dying to have access to the building and to church services. Although this will mean a huge expense ($90,000 to $100,000) and other projects must be postponed, this puts a "new face" on the church's intent to keep members in the embrace of the community as long as they desire. This move was activated by their experience with a member who died recently of AIDS and had to be carried up the steps to the church in his last weeks; he wanted fervently to be in worship up to the end (and managed this until two weeks before he died).

First Presbyterian of Evanston does not carry Eucharist to the dying unless the person requests this. However, a member recently asked for a healing service for his wife, who once had been a Catholic. The pastors joined a group of people whom the husband had invited to anoint the sick woman with oil and to pray. The interpretation of "healing" was broad; although the wife died later that night, all participants felt that the service had touched her, allowing her the peace to die.

At Saint Nicholas, communion is carried to the dying, and the priests and ministry of care anoint the person on the head and palms with oil. Once the church delivered "last rites"; now it is moving toward a more comprehensive understanding of the "art of dying." This summer, five or six were anointed, a practice the priest feels "gives permission to die" and offers a "healing unto death."[19] Dying well seems to require that we honor the dying person's sense of knowing when it is time to fight and when it is time to let go, cherishing whatever gifts are here and now.[20]

Saint Nicholas long ago moved in the direction of keeping the sick and dying not only in the thoughts but also in the presence of the parish. The sick are encouraged to attend Mass as long as they wish. Where those in wheelchairs used to sit at the front of the chapel, now they sit out in the congregation, breaking down the fear and separation between the ill and the well. Parishioners are encouraged to speak up during the service, to call to the parish's attention their own needs or those of others. In the future, the priest hopes to hold a service every Saturday for the anointing of the sick.

Surveys

The responses from our surveys revealed that, in some instances, not only the leader of the faith community but also the laity were actively engaged in the sacramental aspects of dying. Two urban congregations noted that they have a formal sacramental ministry called Ministry of Care, in which "trained and mandated parishioners" bring Eucharist to the sick. Professor Vogel recounts the receiving of Eucharist by an extended family whose elderly parent was dying. The Eucharist, "a foretaste of the banquet table in God's Kingdom," provided a time for remembering, forgiving, and "coming home," for both the dying person and the larger household.[21]

Closings

"It's all in God's hands now."

But is it? Ann Dudley Goldblatt, quoting Bacon, reminds us that "knowledge is power."[22] A critical component of response to the suffering and dying of its members is the idea of the place of worship as a center for gathering and disseminating information. The congregation should be a stimulator and protector of dialogue and advocacy, educating its members about their rights "to be active participants in decisions that affect the quality of their life and choices about treatment and the withholding of treatment" (Professor Vogel). Many congregations, realizing that most Americans are woefully underinformed about their choices at the end of life, have instituted active programs for the education of their members. To lack education about choices is to surrender your freedom and limit your control over the end (and by extension the entire history) of your life. We also have a responsibility to join the public debate on delivery of health care and policies that surround the dying process. Not to do so "grants undue powers to government, to insurance companies, to hospital and nursing homes, and to lawyers, judges, and doctors."[23]

Education

Professor Vogel recalls for us the 1971 United Methodist/Roman Catholic dialogue on faith, death, and dying that issued in *Holy Living & Holy Dying* (1986). This statement offers "pastoral guidance and a format for inviting all faithful persons into dialogue about life and death decisions," for "[p]ersons of faith must enter into the public debate about the making and carrying out of difficult end-of-life decisions; we must bring our commitment to justice, compassion, and wholeness for all persons into the public arena, where we engage in dialogue and advocacy."

The two areas in which educational programs have been most aggressively developed are AIDS awareness and care for the elderly. Lincoln Park Presbyterian, comprised largely of young adults, recently held educational forums on the medical dimensions and personal aspect of AIDS. Juan Alegria of the AIDS Pastoral Network spoke with the congregation. In addition, the pastor encourages honest interchange among members to work on the congregation's "self-awareness and learnings" about AIDS. This year, "John's" partner, "Tom," who now also has AIDS, has participated in the church's educational seminars. He urges members to "take a risk," to speak or interact with someone with AIDS. Persons who are terminally ill need to be able to be with other people; "laughter is deeply healing."

Saint Mark's Episcopal has a ministry to the "sandwich" generation as one of its many educational programs. The rector recommends discussion among parishioners about dying and death issues, instruction about power of attorney or living wills, "so people understand what they're agreeing to, have the option of knowing what they don't want to agree to."[24] The rector stocks pamphlets on services that are available to help persons who are dying. The parish also orchestrates intergenerational programs (e.g., making Advent wreaths and valentines with the children) so that older people are known throughout the community and don't become isolated. When an older member becomes ill and dies, the children feel that they are part of this process; this is their friend.

Congregation Rodfei Zedek in Hyde Park recently held a three-part lecture series on "How a Jew Dies," led by hospi-

tal chaplain Phyllis Tobak. This year Rabbi Tobak will
return to discuss living wills.

Dying is not a generational matter; not only the elderly and
the young single, but also those in the middle years may be
struck down. While Lincoln Park and Saint Vincent's have few
older members in a "revolving door" community of young singles, Beth Emet the Free is comprised largely of multiperson
households, including many men and women with children.
Among the dying have been mothers in their middle years with
children at home. Thus education is tailored to those needs. A
new group forming at Beth Emet the Free, in conjunction with
The Park Ridge Center, is "The Congregation as a Place of
Healing," modeled on the group at Grace Lutheran Church in
River Forest (discussed below) that deals with chronic illness.

Sometimes "education" is provided by the dying person
himself or herself, expanding the "learnings," as Rector Jeff
Doane has said. Reba, which like Lincoln Park is a fairly
young congregation, was taught by one of their older members, a psychiatrist whose wife had recently died.

"[H]e was very intentional about knowing he was dying.
He had cancer and elected not to have more invasive procedures to prolong his life. He felt like he understood what was
coming; it was time to die, and he was ready for it. . . . 'I'm
going to be with Jesus, I'm going to be reunited with my
wife, and I've really finished all my business on earth.' "

The pastor has commented, "[Our real belief is] that we're
going to be with the Lord, meaning that we don't need to
put in an investment to try to prolong life as long as possible." This belief fuels Reba Church's commitment to
encourage people to have a living will, in order not to have
"all those procedures that are expensive and a poor use of
resources. We don't need to fear death."[25] The priest of
Saints Peter and Paul Greek Orthodox Church echoes: "The
person who is in the life of the church doesn't have the horror of death."

A powerful gathering at Grace Lutheran Church that began about ten years ago was the Chronic Illness Group.[26] This group has met about once a month (twice if someone is quite ill) over this time to discuss the reality of dying and death in their own lives, perhaps achieving the "public" nature of the dying process to which Rabbi Wolf has referred as a healing direction for all of us. The group at Grace helps people live with chronic illness but also serves as a resource to the congregation at large. During the years, five members of the group have died; in several cases, the dying person and the group planned the funeral together. One funeral (of a former Roman Catholic) included a "liturgical richness" that has freed the congregation to experiment in other worship and funeral styles; in fact, since that time, it has become common for the dying person, not the pastors alone, to plan the funeral. In another instance, the group offered continued support to a member who wanted to attend church right up to the end, despite multiple diseases and weakness.

"Acting in faith and working on health," the congregational nurse program, offers private health counseling and health promotion, prevention, and education. For instance, the parish nurse at Saint Nicholas offers information on living wills and durable power of attorney, and also provides education for adults and the youth group on AIDS, safe sex, and human sexuality. Recently Father James Bresnahan came to the parish to give a workshop on aging, with case studies; the study group became the "family" in a hands-on involvement with sensitive issues when dealing with the dying elderly. As part of "Novembering," discussed below, the community gathers to reflect on the practical aspects of dying: making of wills, advance directives, planning of funerals.

"Novembering" is the most innovative, yet tradition-based movement to recover the communal and natural aspects of dying—a month-long time of remembrance and celebration, in which the seasons of the year are recalled as the church year draws to its close and begins anew.[27]

> Halloween, All Saints, and All Souls send us back to the paschal images of dying and rising, and forward through a month-long harvest festival to the final in-gathering of God's holy ones at the end of time. . . . Novembering sees the connection and interrelationship of masks and costumes to both the fear of death and the playful challenging of death.[28]

The month begins with an All-Hallow's Eve procession to Mass with the children of the parish in costumes, their banner bearing autumn shades. Throughout the month, votive lights burn and marigolds incense the altar; communicants are urged to bring photos of family and friends who had died, recalling the Hispanic tradition of the Altar of the Departed, from "Dia de Los Muertos."[29] The names of loved ones are inscribed in the *Book of the Names of the Dead* and are read out at Mass. Thus death and life are joined in one "seamless garment."

Surveys

From among the 28 surveys we received, one urban congregation held a six-week session on death and dying which emphasized extraordinary treatment, advance directives, and decision making. Six dealt with death and dying regularly in adult education classes, with one church adding that its greatest concern was with gang-related deaths. An equal number who responded said that the subject of dying was usually dealt with in sermons, often in the wake of a death; the funeral or memorial services often offered what Oldershaw has called a "moment of opportunity" for the congregation to consider dying and death in both spiritual and practical ways. Almost all the religious bodies that have no current programs expressed the desire to see "organized effort," with help from the outside, to learn how to deal "more sensitively" with these issues—for instance, a "dialogue on ethical issues of rationing health care and assisted death," and more dissemination of information about advance directives.

Formal support groups for the dying were less common, with one urban church offering a six-week class with a maximum of twelve people. The format is fixed, and the series is offered twice a year. One church is currently planning a support group. Another has a women's support group, and yet another states that it "provides no such support groups," as individuals are referred to hospitals and other care centers that do provide them. Most of the respondents felt that there was no need for support groups, as their congregation was small, or had more young than old members, or that the needs of the dying were adequately handled by the priest, pastor, rabbi, or deacons. A number lean on groups related to hospice. Two of the 28 respondents noted that their congregations were plagued by "significant levels of gang violence and death" affecting young people, and that they needed help with this. To assist with this problem, one congregation participates in the interfaith monthly candlelight vigil against violence in their community.

Professor Linda Vogel's words summarize the attitude of faith communities as they attempt to be faithful to God and to the needs of their constituents:

> Suffering and dying can be transformed by faith and hope for those who are dying, and for those who walk with them through the "shadow of the valley of death" (Psalm 23). We call for open dialogue and advocacy for the rights of persons to be active participants in decisions that affect the quality of their life, and choices about treatment and the withholding of treatment. We call communities of faith to examine their ways of nurturing, caring, teaching, and creating and celebrating liturgies with persons who are dying, and with their families and friends.[30]

− Coda −

Reflections

We close with the reflections of Professor Robert Jewett, distinguished scholar, churchman, and public servant, but also child, a son who asks how we can "die well" when our machines and nature deny this to us.[1]

During the last decade, my parents and my wife's parents died—three of Alzheimer's and one of senile dementia. Reflecting on their passing—especially the peculiar form of their passing before they died—from a biblical perspective, drawing together meditations and speeches for each of the deaths for the sake of the family, I find myself thinking about the problems that form of death presents. My mother was in a vegetative state for about eight years, and my father was in a vegetative state for the last two or three months. All four parents experienced, at the end of their lives, a loss of selfhood and a peculiar phenomenon which I can call only dying before death. In these particular cases, death came too late.

The vision of nineteenth-century religionists, embodied in what was one of the most popular storytelling and narrative forms at the time, was the deathbed narrative story of a great Christian saint—Aunt Susan, who would gather her family about her at age 83, recount her life of service to the community, embody the prayers of the community, and die with a heavenly vision, after advising the grandchildren on

134

how to properly live their lives. That kind of narrative, which of course totally died out during the twentieth century, had been a major form of storytelling and Christian literature—several Christian periodicals contained a story like that every month—"sustaining people in the good death."

But in the case of Alzheimer's patients, there is no good death. In fact, the experience of the families of Alzheimer's patients is that of relief when death comes. The peculiar impact on families of Alzheimer's patients and people caught in senile dementia is that their memories are blocked. My memory was blocked for a period of four years because this vegetative person was not the person I knew and loved. Death, in all four instances, suddenly released memory, allowing families to recall the wonderful services—the wonderful generativity—of each of these four people whose lives of service had been invisible to the family and the community for a very long time, leading me to reflect on the impact of that form of extended dying, which I think is a peculiar feature of the twentieth century. People in the nineteenth century simply did not receive the level of care that permits such patients to last as long as they are currently lasting. What impact, of course, has this numbing of memory and loss of respect for the past, particularly in the case of the grandchildren, who for almost a decade experienced their grandparents as people without wit, without energy, without generativity? In all four cases, the grandchildren were stunned at the funerals to hear accounts of the rich lives of these four people, and somehow seeing them end in such an undignified state cut back on their sense of respect for the past. In the case of my mother and father—especially my mother—an even more serious problem surfaced in my mind, and I still can't get over it.

When my parents, who were from upstate New York, came to the World's Fair in Chicago, by train of course (my mother and father were conservative Methodists with no tradition of cremation in their families), they passed by miles and miles of cemeteries. My mother came to the very strong moral sense that it was somehow wrong to fill the earth with graves. She, then in her thirties, became the first member of her family to be committed to cremation for the sake of the preservation of the earth. In all four cases—my wife's family in schools and church leadership, and my parents in preaching and church leadership—the commitment to productivity was combined with this moral sense that they should contribute during their life and by what means they had left over. My parents wanted to give to their college. Of course, that life dream—the end of the generativity commitment—was frustrated completely by the form of death that both experienced, which neither would have chosen. The sad thing about Alzheimer's and dementia is that the person is beyond choosing. The self-chosen death is no longer a possibility. This leads to a final set of thoughts that have been ruminating in my mind, relating to the contrast between that form of death and the considerably more dignified Native American forms of death.

I'm a Great Plains person from Nebraska, and the stories of the plains Indians are in the front of my mind. There we have the double experience of older people deciding that they are no longer generative for the tribe, that their time has come. They move away from the tribe to an isolated location and begin singing a death chant. Particularly relevant is the fact that they stop taking nourishment—they will not drink, and they will not eat. Apparently there is no sense of hunger or thirst and, singing the death chant, within one or two days death comes.

I think of my father-in-law, who was a great civic leader for whom the early onset of Alzheimer's was a spatial dislocation. He would have been a chief, but as he began to fall into Alzheimer's, he clearly would have been lost as a plains Indian. He would have drifted off in the wintertime in a blizzard or when hunting. He didn't have the capacity to find his way home. A natural death would have come, and that tribe never would have seen George Miller in the disoriented state into which he was gradually drifting toward the end of his career. This leads me to wonder whether there is a moral logic, a moral voice in the brain stem? What is it that leads Alzheimer's patients to cease demanding food and cease wanting it?

In the case of my mother, we made the unwise choice to not sign the papers, and she was force-fed for an eight-year period. She no longer demanded food but was kept in a vegetative state, with my family visiting and my father visiting every day. I had a very firm experience of this when visiting my father a few weeks before his death. He was in dementia but had fallen into a sleep state, from which he no longer awoke nor wanted food and water. The nurses, of course, as responsible as they were, were waking him up on schedule and taking him in for meals. I had the strongest impression that his brain stem was saying: "I don't want to drink—I don't want to eat anymore—I want to sing that death chant all by myself." In the last twenty-four to forty-eight hours of his life, my family's urge that he not be awakened was followed, and he fell into a very peaceful, quiet death—the only one of the four parents who died with a measure of dignity at the very end.

As I reflect, I wonder about the quality of mercy. Is it mercy, perhaps, in such cases, to renounce power, to allow natural processes to advance? Would it be possible for us to recapture some of the dignity of that natural form of self-imposed death of our Native American forebears, which did not require the intervention of their tribes when they felt their time of generativity was over; which allowed a process that gives a signal to the brain stem to allow thirst no longer to act as a raging voice, but allows the body to die in a dignified way?

[handwritten note] ↳ ↑ v defines Quality of Life only as it contributes

– LEADER'S GUIDE –

"I went to my father's wake expecting terror and misery. What a surprise it was to experience celebration instead, from his many friends who had gathered."

We in the Center for Ethics offer a thesis for exploring what it means to die well in the late twentieth century. In our own explorations, we have sought to define a good death in terms of biological, psychological, social, and theological parameters. It is the definition of *shalom* or *agape*:

> Dying well is to end one's days in old age, relieved of pain,
> surrounded by one's friends and family,
> attended by sensitive caregiving,
> reconciled with all persons,
> in justice with humanity and the world, at peace with God.

It would be well to post this definition in full view of the class to keep the discussions oriented on the central issue: What it means to "die well" in the face of constant stalls and assaults on that seemingly natural and humanistic hope.

These discussions can be structured for either a six-week or an eight-week course. The general design is for the class to consider, at the outset of each hour-long session, the questions posed at the beginning of each chapter, reading and discussing with these in mind. We suggest that you initiate discussion by selecting one passage from the chapter to unravel, then move to a consideration of the overall argument of the chapter, to keep focused on the particulars of each problem that complicates "dying well."

The two "codas" are written as possible test cases for the review and analysis of material in the three chapters that preceded them. You will notice, however, that in each coda, what might seem to offer some "solutions" in fact may pose additional questions, requiring the nuanced positioning of ethical determinations suggested by some of the chapter questions. In particular, the second coda, which appears at the end of the book, presents real and quite recent case studies of the way even spiritually sensitive persons who, when they are healthy, would say that they understand the meaning of their death and can provide for peace during their dying, can be swept away by events, or (in the case of the eight-year coma) be blind-sided by an unexpected and greatly undesired process of dying. At the end of the course, you may wish members of the class to share their own painful or joyful experiences with the dying and death of a member of their household or a friend.

We recommend that your class members read all or parts of Quill's and Nuland's books; the medical language, the immediacy of the clinical environment, will help the class avoid sentimentality and construct positive models.[1] In our presentations in this guide, we have tried to be true to the seriousness of the problems in all areas—societal, medical, and theological—while testifying to the positive spirit that has animated the various disciplines (we think here particularly of the professions most under fire—law and medicine). In Quill and Nuland (and the other physicians who participated in our study—van Eys, Franklin, Oldershaw, et al.), we want to acknowledge the tremendous power to reform and humanize, to recapture the original energy of medicine and law to honor and protect the vulnerable, which currently animates the practice of those professions.

Theology, and theologies, also come under scrutiny as disciplines, professions, and systems of belief. Here, too, we hope to shape the dialogue within as broad a frame as possible. For instance, in chapter 3, we wrap the overall presentation of the theological settings in the glorious colors of Laurie's suffering and death, and therefore usually refer to Christian understandings (she was a Roman Catholic). However, the models of "death as friend," "death as enemy," and "generosity" as ways to interpret human response to dying and death are ancient and persistent. The Christian responses can be best understood in the context of Judaism, with its passionate interpretation of "righteousness" as the obligation of one person to honor and care for the other, and for members individually of a society to care for the larger body political, the larger social context in which all have their life. Further, both Christianity and Judaism were fired in the crucible of the ancient Near East, drawing richly from the religions and belief systems in the societies that lived around them.

What does all this portend? That we approach these monumental questions with respect—in awe that we find ourselves so overwhelmed by the creatures and constructs of our own human imaginings but with gratitude that we have the intelligence to recognize our dilemmas, courage to face them, and compassion enough to convene for some hours, some months, to offer our solutions for them. In so doing, we join the many in law, in technology, in economics, in medicine, in theology—and in congregations of many faiths—to ask the hard questions of one another and of ourselves.

– Notes –

Part One: Basic Issues

1. Washington, D.C.: National Academy Press, 1995, ch. 21.

Chapter 1: The Social Setting

1. See C. Margaret McClaskey, "Survivors: How Do They Die?" in *Ethos: Proceedings of the Center for Ethics*, Vol. 1 (forthcoming).
2. James F. Breshnahan, S.J., is professor of medical ethics and codirector of the medical ethics and humanities program at Northwestern University Medical School in Chicago. His 1994 talk on contemporary *ars moriendi*, the inaugural lecture for the Center for Ethics, was taken in part from "The Catholic Art of Dying," which appears in the revised edition of the *Encyclopedia of Bioethics* (New York: Macmillan, 1995). His April 28, 1995, lecture on faith and ethics in the Catholic tradition appears in fuller form in *America* (November 4, 1995), pp. 12-16. For further development of his ideas, see "Observations on the Rejection of Physician-Assisted Suicide: a Roman Catholic Perspective," in *Christian Bioethics: Non-ecumenical Studies in Medical Morality* (Vol. I, No. 3, 1995), pp. 256-84.

Chapter 2: The Medical Setting

1. "Death and Dignity: A Case of Individualized Decision Making."
2. Ibid. Quill's book on the subject is *Death and Dignity: Making Choices and Taking Charge* (New York: W. W. Norton, 1993).
3. Dr. van Eys has "gone on record against euthanasia and assisted suicide." Dr. van Eys, keynote speaker at the Center for Ethics conferences May 25, 1994, and April 28, 1995, is Clinical Professor of Pediatrics at Vanderbilt University School of Medicine. His two papers, "Assisted Suicide and Euthanasia" and "The Dark Side of Human Mercy," which present full and nuanced analyses of the complex facets of these issues, will appear in full in the first volume of *Ethos: Proceedings of the Center for Ethics* (forthcoming).
4. Nuland's reference is to Quill's *Death and Dignity*. We recommend both Quill and Nuland as companions to the study guide. See also Richard Momeyer, *Confronting Death* (Bloomington, Ind.: Indiana University Press, 1988), and Kenneth L. Vaux, *Death Ethics: Religious and Cultural Values in Prolonging and Ending Life* (Philadelphia: Trinity Press International, 1992).
5. Quill, p. 22.
6. Franklin J. Miller and Howard Brody, "Professional Integrity and Physician-Assisted Death," *Hastings Center Report*, May-June, 1995, pp. 8 ff.
7. Timothy E. Quill and Christine K. Cassel, "Nonabandonment: A Central Obligation for Physicians," *Annals of Internal Medicine* 122 (March 1, 1995), 368-74.
8. Francis Moore, "Prolonging Life, Permitting Life to End," *Harvard Magazine* (July-August 1995), pp. 46-47.
9. Recently, Dr. Kevorkian has been exonerated in several of his euthanasia cases, and physician-assisted suicide prohibition legislation has been found unconstitutional by a Federal Appeals Court in San Francisco.

Chapter 3: The Theological Setting

1. W. H. Auden, "For the Time Being," *The Collected Poems* (New York: Random House, © renewed 1968 by W. H. Auden).
2. The theology of dying and death in Judaism will be discussed in the paper by Rabbi Dr. Byron Sherwin, "Death and Dying in Jewish Tradition," to appear in the first volume of *Ethos*. Rabbi Sherwin is Verson Professor of Jewish Philosophy and Mysticism and Vice-President for Academic Affairs, Spertus Institute of Jewish Studies, Chicago. See also David M. Feldman, *Health and Medicine in the Jewish Tradition: L'Hayyim—to Life* (New York: Crossroad, 1986), in the series *Health/Medicine and the Faith Traditions*, eds. Martin E. Marty and Kenneth L. Vaux. Some flavor of how other faith traditions view dying and death can be seen in the report prepared by Catherine L. Vaux, which also will appear in *Ethos*.
3. J. D. Crossan, *The Historical Jesus: The Life of a Mediterranean Jewish Peasant* (San Francisco: Harper, 1991); E. P. Saunders, *Jesus and Judaism* (Philadelphia: Fortress, 1989).
4. In his paper delivered at the Kellogg Conference on April 28, 1995, Rabbi Sherwin responded to both poles of thought—the death-deniers and the death-obsessors: "Judaism never has avoided either the inevitability or the reality of death. . . . The proclivity to deny, to repress, or to escape death, has neither been a feature of Jewish faith nor of Jewish historical experience. . . . Unlike the cults of death that characterized ancient Egyptian religion, and unlike the Babylonian Gilgamesh, who vainly strives to discover eternal life, the primary directive of Hebrew Scriptures is the challenge of sanctifying life, rather than escaping or being preoccupied with death."
5. Oscar Cullmann, "Immortality of the Soul or Resurrection of the Death," in Krister Stendahl, ed., *Immortality and Resurrection* (New York: Macmillan, 1965), p. 19.
6. Sherwin (see note 4).

Coda: Exploring Some Solutions

1. Michael Hyde was formerly McCormick Distinguished Professor of Rhetoric at Northwestern University. He is now the J. Tylee Wilson Professor of Business Ethics, Dept. of Speech Communications at Wake Forest University. His major publication on this subject is "Medicine, Rhetoric, and Euthanasia: A Case Study in the Workings of a Postmodern Discourse," in *Quarterly Journal of Speech* 79 (1993: 201-24).
2. All quotations are taken from a transcript of Hyde's lecture at the Center for Ethics, March 14, 1994, "The Rhetoric of Euthanasia."
3. The lectures of both Goldblatt and Wiet will appear in the first volume of *Ethos*. Ann Dudley Goldblatt is Senior Lecturer, Social Sciences and Humanities Collegiate Divisions, University of Chicago. Mitchell J. Wiet is Vice-President and Legal Counsel, Northwestern Memorial Hospital, Chicago.
4. *Setting Limits: Medical Goals in an Aging Society* (Georgetown University Press, 1995).
5. Ibid., pp. 181-82.
6. Callahan. "Pursuing a Peaceful Death," in *Hastings Center Report*, Vol. 23, No. 4 (July-August 1993), p. 33. This article is taken from ch. 6 of *The Troubled Dream of Life* (New York: Simon & Schuster, 1993).

7. Ibid., p. 34.
8. Ibid., p. 36.

Part Two: Case Studies

1. The studies to which we refer are Aaron Kerr, "Death and Distance: How We Kill and Die in Prison"; C. Margaret McClaskey, "Survivors: How Do They Die?"; Robert B. Campbell, "Ethical Decision-Making and Advanced Medical Intervention"; and Eddie O. Dixon, "Healing Actions: The Aftermath of the Violent Death of Children." These papers will appear in full in the first volume of *Ethos*. A fifth study, "Home and Habitat in Dying well: Case Study Armenia" deals with dislocation and removal of topological and psychological supports that might ease dying.

Chapter 4: Societal Response

1. Based on the Kellogg Foundation project of the same name by Glenn Brichacek, presented April 29, 1995. A full version of the paper will appear in the first volume of *Ethos*.
2. Professor Bonnie Miller-McLemore of the Divinity School, Vanderbilt University, discusses "disregard for caregivers and dependents" at length in her essay "Dying Well Against the Odds: Cultural and Religious Horizons." The "underside of caregiving," she writes, is that the patient would die without the feeding, cleaning, and bodily comfort provided by the mother, child, or hired helper, and this service is poorly compensated, inadequately recognized. "Caring for others requires other people and institutions standing by. A caregiver (mother or adult child) cannot survive unless that giving is refreshed by the supportive attentions of another, whether spouse, neighbor, friend, or relative." Miller-McLemore's essay, delivered April 28, 1995, appears in full in the first volume of *Ethos*.
3. Brichacek cites Donald Heinz, "Finishing the Story: Aging, Spirituality, and the Work of Culture," *Journal of Religious Gerontology*, 1994, pp. 9, 3-18, and T. Patrick Hill & David Shirley, *A Good Death* (Reading, Mass.: Addison-Wesley Publishing Co., 1992).
4. Interview, Vivekananda Vendanta Society, Hyde Park, Ill., July 25, 1994.
5. Interview, Lisa Cortez, Wilmette, Ill., July 21, 1994.
6. All quotes in "Religion and Dying Well in the Nursing Home" are from Brichacek's text in *Ethos* (forthcoming) unless otherwise indicated.
7. Brichacek cites H. G. Koenig, D. O. Moberg, and J. N. Kvale, "Religious and Health Characteristics of Patients Attending a Geriatric Assessment Clinic," *Journal of American Geriatrics Society*, 1988, pp. 36, 362-73, and Koenig, *Aging and God* (New York: Haworth Pastoral Press, 1993).
8. Brichacek cites work of C. D. Batson and W. L. Ventis, *The Religious Experience* (New York: Oxford University Press, 1982), p. 1952, and their later work in 1993. Intrinsic religion he later defines as "the form of religion that internally motivates an individual to live out her or his faith" and extrinsic, "the use of religion for self-serving purposes."
9. Subjects were fully informed of the nature of this study before they agreed to participate.
10. The Family Leave Act has certainly helped in some cases, as one difficulty in

providing home attention lies with the working status of many women. A dying parent cannot be left alone, but firms, or even supposedly supportive agencies such as universities, have not honored the employee's wish to take time out to care for an elderly parent.

11. Confucius, *The Book of Filial Duty*, trans. Ivan Chen (New York: E. P. Dutton, 1910), ch. 1.
12. Cha's work, presented at the Kellogg conference at the Center for Ethics April 29, 1995, will appear in the first volume of *Ethos*. All quotes in "Dying Within the Household" are from Cha's text unless otherwise indicated.
13. Confucius, *Analects*, trans. James Legge (New York: Dover, 1971). This is a republished, unabridged edition of the second revised edition as published by Clarendon Press (Oxford, 1893). An earlier reference to James Legge's translation appears as 1891, published by J. B. Alden.
14. Drew Christiansen, "Aging and the Aged: Ethical Implication in Aging," *Encyclopedia of Bioethics*, ed. Warren T. Reich (New York: Free Press, 1978), Vol. 1, 61-2.
15. Kwang Chung Kim, Shin Kim, and Won Moo Hurh, "Filial Piety and Intergenerational Relationship in Korean Immigrant Families," *International Journal of Aging and Human Development*, Vol. (3), 236.
16. Jong Min Lee, "The Mission of the Senior Citizen in the Immigrant Community." D. Min. dissertation, McCormick Theological Seminary, 1986, p. 5.
17. Cha, summarizing the work of Donald Gelland, *Aging: The Ethnic Factor* (Boston: Little, Brown & Co., 1982), p. 52.
18. Cha, reporting on conversations with "Rev. Kim," the pastor of his church, who had been a social worker among Korean Americans for years.
19. Cha, summarizing Kim.

Chapter 5: Health Care Responses

1. Dr. Kathy Neely, summary of her Kellogg Foundation project "Early Encounters with Death: Narrative Reflections of the First Year Medical Students." This project was presented April 29, 1995. A full text will appear in the first volume of *Ethos*. All quotes in "Humanizing Medical Training" are from Neely's paper unless otherwise indicated.
2. As most of us will recognize, many medical schools have moved in directions similar to those Dr. Neely proposes: Wisconsin, for instance, introduces students to clinics in their first year; Pritzker (University of Chicago) incorporates clinical experience early on, and also is one of many schools that require an ethics component in education; and Harvard, whose innovative program of education has been a focus on the news for some years and is similarly designed to enhance and preserve the prospective physicians' human sensitivities.
3. Dr. Franklin's paper, prepared for the Kellogg Foundation project and presented April 29, 1995, will appear in full in the first volume of *Ethos*. All quotes in "Humanizing the ICU" are from Dr. Franklin's text unless otherwise indicated.
4. Nuland, p. 254.
5. See Franklin's full discussion in *Ethos*.
6. Professor Bonnie Miller-McLemore adds this dimension to Dr. Franklin's emphasis on the need for patient comfort: "Not only is physical pain difficult to manage, other forms of suffering—including the existential afflictions of

the soul—almost always baffle the caregiver." Perhaps we have set up physicians to "do our dirty work, to carry the burdens of society and essentially fill in for lost family, lost religion, lost faith." From Miller-McLemore's lecture, "Dying Well Against the Odds: Cultural and Religious Horizons," in the first volume of *Ethos*.

7. Franklin. "Fraction" refers to the loss of blood flow capacity in the heart.
8. Franklin, quoting Bean.
9. Dr. Franklin reminds us, however, of the Karen Quinlan case, where the expected death did not occur when life supports were removed.
10. Inability to breathe; gasping for breath.
11. While what Franklin describes here is not "mercy-killing," fears on the part of staff and physicians that they might somehow be participating in mercy-killing are real concerns that must be addressed. Hence the need for strict guidelines and the need, too, of the cautionary words of Dr. Jan van Eys that we should "treat all alike, with humility, and tenderness to your suffering fellow human. . . . There is a great chasm between tenderness in humility and mercy out of power." From "The Dark Side of Human Mercy." See also note 3, chapter 2.
12. Franklin, here and in the discussion to follow.
13. However, note Dr. Franklin's recommendations that we not place terminally ill patients in ICU.
14. This fear surfaced repeatedly in all our studies, including those not reviewed in this guide: dying in a special care facility such as for the ventilator-dependent; dying now after having been left for dead during wartime, as with Holocaust survivors; dying "on the road," as with the Armenian genocide; dying on the street, as with violent deaths of young Americans. "Who will be there to hold my hand when I die?"
15. Dr. Oldershaw's paper of the same name, prepared for the Kellogg Foundation project and presented April 29, 1995, will appear in full in the first volume of *Ethos*.
16. Oldershaw, quoting Nuland, *How We Die*, p. 258.
17. Oldershaw, drawing on T. S. Mappes and J. M. Zembaty, *Biomedical Ethics*, 3rd ed. (New York: McGraw-Hill, 1991).
18. As he digested the results of his study, Dr. Oldershaw recognized that the legal component in this relationship has become increasingly complicated by "insurers' emphasis on reduction of medical costs, rather than on providing the highest available quality of care," and the problems of conflict of interest in referral cases.
19. Dr. Siegel's paper, "Dying Well in Cancer: Global Management of the Cancer Patient," which contains a great deal more scientific detail than we can present here, will appear in full in the first volume of *Ethos*. All quotes in "Global Management" are from Siegel's texts.

Chapter 6: Religious Responses

1. The questionnaire was developed by Catherine L. Vaux, in consultation with Professor Linda Vogel. Ms. Vaux, a graduate of the University of Chicago, conducted the interviews and analyzed the data. Her findings will appear in Vol. I of *Ethos*.
2. Interview, September 1, 1994. Rabbi Wolf serves KAM Isaiah Israel Congregation in Hyde Park, Ill.

3. Summary of paper of Professor Linda Vogel, "Ministry with the Living and the Dying through Education, Liturgy, Nurture, and Advocacy," which will appear in full in the first volume of *Ethos*.
4. Interview with Rabbi Peter Knobel, September 7, 1995.
5. Interview with Pastor Fred Sindorf, August 2, 1994.
6. Interview with Pastor Sally Schreiner, August 1, 1994.
7. Phone interview with Rabbi Wolf, September 1, 1995.
8. This program has been developed by Jan Shephardson, RN, board member at the Center for Ethics and a long-time director of the hospice.
9. Interview with the Rev. Judith Watt, September 7, 1995. Rev. Watt, like the other religious leaders we interviewed, is aware that lay ministries do not always satisfy all parishioners, particularly as death is near. She and the other ministers are ready to meet with anyone who so desires.
10. The parish or congregational nurse program grew out of Granger Westberg's long-time commitment to holistic health concerns. The program at St. Francis Hospital, which now has seven nurses based in congregations in the area, began its Visiting Nurse program in 1987.
11. Interview with Fr. Robert Oldershaw and Mary Signatur, RN, August 29, 1995.
12. September 7, 1995.
13. *Gemeinde* is the ancient term for congregation, which connotes not strictly those who attend services but those too who consider themselves members of a broader community.
14. Perhaps by asking church elders who are no longer in active service to take communion to the dying after each Communion Sunday.
15. This "forthright attitude toward the reality of death" is "bluntly articulated in the liturgical deathbed confessional," writes Rabbi Byron Sherwin. He quotes from the confessional: "Both my cure and my death are in your hands . . . if my death is determined by You, I accept it at Your hand. Into Your hands I commend my spirit." From "Death and Dying in Jewish Tradition."
16. Ibid.
17. Rabbi Wolf, 1994.
18. Interview with Rector Kate Guistolise, July 19, 1994.
19. Fr. Oldershaw. Fr. Jim Kastigar is also involved with the anointing of the dying as well as with education and other parish duties.
20. See Vogel's text in *Ethos*.
21. Vogel.
22. Professor Goldblatt's lecture, "Closing the Circle," delivered at the Kellogg Foundation conference April 28, 1995, will appear in full in the first volume of *Ethos*.
23. Vogel.
24. Rector Guistolise.
25. Pastor Schreiner.
26. This group is now under the mantle of the Park Ridge Center, which grew out of Project Ten. Project Ten (the short name for "Health/Medicine and the Faith Traditions") was begun by Kenneth L. Vaux in 1978, in discussion with Larry Holst and others from the Clinical Pastoral Care department at Lutheran General Hospital. University of Chicago Divinity School professor Martin E. Marty joined Vaux in 1980, as together they sought to "assist the inquiry of all who seek deeper understanding in order to decide about issues of

health and disease in the light of beliefs and values." From the Introduction to *Health/Medicine and the Faith Traditions: An Inquiry into Religion and Medicine*, eds. Martin E. Marty and Kenneth L. Vaux (Philadelphia: Fortress Press, 1982), p. ix.

27. Those interested in exploring this idea further may read Fr. Oldershaw's article in *GIA Quarterly* (Summer 1995), Vol. 6, No. 4, pp. 8-12: "Novembering." Co-authored with Christine Neff and Timothy Estberg.

28. Ibid., p. 8.

29. St. Nicholas has recently been joined by a now-defunct largely Hispanic parish in Chicago, which has shared its rich cultural traditions with its new fellow parishioners.

30. Summary of Kellogg Foundation project presentation.

Coda: Reflections

1. These reflections were shared as "Caring for Elderly Parents: A Personal View" at the Kellogg Foundation conference, April 28, 1995. This text is taken from a transcript of Professor Jewett's remarks.

Leader's Guide

1. Quill, *Death and Dignity;* Nuland, *How We Die.*